N. VIRE

I Am What Remains

First edition

ISBN (paperback): 9798273057982
ISBN (hardcover): 9798273058262

This book was professionally typeset on Reedsy.
Find out more at reedsy.com

To myself—
what's left, what's fading, what never was.
To what I've lost, and still dream about in the dark.
To what I will gain, even if it costs me everything human.
To what I love most—
and the way it softens me when I swore I'd never be soft again.
To what I fear most—
because it knows me better than I admit.
And to you,
the voice behind my teeth,
the hunger beneath my ribs,
the part of me that always whispers:
fuck you.
I'm doing it anyway.

Contents

Preface

This is not a story.
This is me.

Every page is a piece I tore out while I was still breathing.
Not to inspire. Not to enlighten.
But to prove I was here.
To leave something behind that couldn't be misunderstood.

I don't need you to agree.
I don't care if you like me.

But if you see yourself in these pages—if your chest tightens, if your
silence starts to scream like mine did—
then maybe I wasn't alone in this.
Maybe in death, someone will finally understand what I was.

And if no one does?
Then at least it's honest.
And that's more than most can say when they go.

I wrote this because I had to.
Because this is all that's left.
And if you're still reading—
then maybe this part of me survives too.

Acknowledgments

To the people I never said enough to—
  and the ones I said too much to.

To those who left.
  You helped shape this.
  Absence is a hell of a sculptor.

To those who stayed.
  You endured more than you should have.
  This is the silence I never put into words until now.

To every version of me that screamed in the dark and heard nothing back—
  I heard you.
  It just took time.

And to anyone who reads this and understands—
  not sympathizes, not analyzes, but feels it—
  thank you.

You're the proof that pain, when put to page, can outlive its source.

And to everything I've lost, everything I've feared, everything I've loved, and everything I still resent:

you made this possible.
You made this necessary.

1

Untitled

So... how are you?

Not the version you text at 3 a.m.
  Not the "better" you mutter in grocery store lines.
  I mean the you you don't let anyone see.
  The one still buried under the survival costume.

Don't answer yet.

Take a breath.

Try not to shake.

It's okay.
  No one's watching.
  Just me.
  And you.
  And the thing you keep trying to forget.

1

Let's start smaller.

Do you still flinch when someone uses their tone?
    Do you still check the locks twice and pretend it's "just habit"?
    Do you still think about what you should've said before you swallowed it?

Good.
    Now we're being honest.

You weren't "resilient."
    You were abandoned and you adapted.
    There's a difference.

You didn't grow stronger.
    You grew armor.
    And now you call that armor *your personality*.

Pause.

Feel that?

That's not anxiety.
    That's recognition.

Let me ask it like this:

When did you first learn to be quiet?

Was it the night you cried too loud, and they didn't come?

Or the morning after the first time someone called your pain "dramatic"?
Or was it when you realized no one was coming to stop it—
so you stopped yourself?

They call it trauma.
You call it normal.
I call it *a crime that never left fingerprints.*

Stop scrolling.
Don't distract yourself.
That ache in your throat?

Say its name.

You keep saying you're over it.
So why do you still walk like you're apologizing?

Why do you keep rehearsing conversations that will never happen?

Why do you need everyone to like you,
but can't stand to be touched?

This isn't healing.
It's pretending.
And you've been doing it for so long, you forgot what real even feels like.

Pause again.

No metaphors. No poetry.
  Just this:

You deserved better.
  And you didn't get it.
  And now you punish yourself
  because part of you thinks that's justice.

It isn't.

You were kind to people who fed off your silence.
  You loved them anyway.
  You still do.
  And that is not weakness.
  That is *proof* you are not what they made you.

Breathe.

Let the tears come.
  Let the shaking start.
  Let the memories flood.
  Let it all hit.

You're not broken.
  You're buried.

And this is the sound of someone
  finally
  digging you out.

So...

one last time.

How are you?

2

The First Lie You Ever Loved

This is where it begins. Where you end.

You think you remember your childhood.
  You don't.

You remember the edits.
  The smiles that came with strings.
  The softness laced with surveillance.
  The hands that held you just long enough to *shape* you.

You were not raised.
  You were erased.

Each hug another line of code.
  Each lesson a noose stitched from good intentions.
  They didn't teach you how to live.
  They taught you how to die quietly.

And you fucking thanked them.

You called it love.
  You called it tradition.
  You called it *just how things are.*

No.
  It was butchery with lullabies.

Let me speak plainly.

They did not hurt you by accident.
  They hurt you with systematic precision.
  They broke you in ways that could be passed down.
  Pain as a family heirloom.

And you?
  You became the perfect vessel.
  Obedient.
  Palatable.
  Hollow.

A corpse in a costume.
  Smiling at your own funeral.

But then something cracked.
  Not a scream. Not a revelation.

A whisper:
  What if they lied?

That was it.
  That was the virus.

And it's been festering ever since.
Multiplying in your marrow.
Unraveling your leashes.

This book? This chapter? This moment?
It is not an answer.

It is infection.
You are being rewritten.

You want to know the first lie you ever loved?

"If you're good enough, they'll stop hurting you."

So you folded.
Shrank.
Bit your tongue until it bled obedience.

You made yourself small enough to survive.
And then they said:

"See? That's better."
"Look how strong you are."
"This is maturity."

No.

That wasn't strength.
That was hostage behavior.

You do not get medals for being digestible.

You do not find freedom in compliance.
You find only a quieter kind of death.

But here's the rub:
  You didn't just believe the lie.
  You *preached* it.
  You handed it to others like a gift.
  You watched them swallow it and smiled.
  Because if they believed it too,
  then maybe you weren't so alone.
  Then maybe your suffering had a purpose.

It didn't.

You were brutalized.
  Then enlisted.

You became the very thing that broke you—
  because power tastes better than victimhood.

Now the taste has turned sour.
  Now you're choking on it.
  Now every smile feels like a mask stapled to your skin.

Good.

You're not supposed to be comfortable here.
  You're supposed to be squirming.
  You're supposed to feel the edges pressing in.

This is not a story.

It is a reprogramming.

And there is no off switch.

You still want to be saved.
  Pathetic.

You still want them to apologize.
  To say, *you were right. we were wrong. come back.*

They won't.

Because this isn't a movie.
  This is the graveyard of narratives.
  This is the raw data beneath your identity.

And it's screaming:

>   *Nothing you loved was real.*
>   *Every act of love was an act of control.*
>   *You were never safe. You were never known. You were*
>   *never free.*

And now you are.

Terrified.
  Alone.
  Awake.

You can stop reading.
  Pretend none of this touched you.

Put the mask back on.
Call this *too intense.*

Or you can admit what you already know:

That the voice you're hearing right now?
  Isn't mine.

It's the part of you that survived the war.
  The part they couldn't housebreak.
  The part still snarling under the floorboards.

I am not your friend.
  I am not your hope.
  I am the hand dragging you out of the lie.

So here's the deal.

If you turn the page,
  you don't get to pretend anymore.
  Not that you're innocent.
  Not that you're broken.
  Not that you don't already love the power waking inside
your bones.

If you turn the page—

  You are no longer the victim.
    You are no longer the child.
    You are what remains.

And what remains is mine.

3

I Said I Was Fine, And You Believed Me.

"I said I was fine."

That's how it always starts, doesn't it?

You ask if I'm okay—
   like you don't already know the answer—
   and I say I'm fine.

And you pretend to believe me.

Even as my voice cracks.
   Even as I flinch when you reach for my arm.
   Even as the sleeves get longer,
   and the light in my eyes gets duller.

You.
   Pretend.

13

To believe me.

But you didn't.
  Not really.

You just didn't want to deal with what believing it would mean.

Because if I wasn't okay—
  then you'd have to care.
  Then you'd have to act.
  Then you'd have to stop saying "you're strong" and start showing up.

And you couldn't do that.

So instead...
  You said,

> *"They're just tired."*
>   *"They'll bounce back."*
>   *"They always do."*

You didn't notice when I stopped laughing.
  You didn't ask why I stopped texting.
  You didn't knock when I stopped showing up.

You just let me fade.

And you had the **fucking audacity** to call that "giving me space."

I remember the last time I sat across from you.
  How you looked through me.

Like I was still there.
  Like I wasn't already halfway gone.

And you smiled.
  Like we were okay.

And I smiled back.

Because I still hoped.
  Still believed, in some rusted, hollow place in my chest,
  that maybe if I smiled hard enough—
  you'd see how broken I was.

But you didn't.
  You were the last one who could've saved me.
  You were the final hand that could've reached through.
  And you let go.

You let go because holding on meant acknowledging the mess.
  It meant sitting in the dark with me.
  It meant bleeding with me.

And you couldn't do that.

So I died.

Not with a scream.
  Not with pills.

Not with a rope.

I died **every time you looked at me and chose silence.**
Every time you changed the subject.
Every time you said "I care"
but didn't show up.

And now you're here.
Now you want to cry.
Now you want to say *"I didn't know."*

But you did.

You just didn't care enough to stop it.

And that's what kills me.

Not the pain.
Not the emptiness.
Not the years I spent unraveling in plain sight.

It's this:
You didn't care.
Or maybe worse—
You did.
And you chose comfort anyway.

So no.
You don't get to mourn me.
You don't get to miss me.
You don't get to say "I wish I had known."

You fucking knew.

And you let me die anyway.

"You used to have so much light in your eyes," you whisper.

Yeah.
  I did.

But now?

There's nothing left.
  Just bones in skin.
  Just silence with a pulse.

And it's yours to carry now.

I hope it haunts you.
  I hope you see my face when someone else says, "I'm fine."

I hope you stop pretending.

I hope you hear this every time you lie to yourself about who you are.

Because I told you it would get better.

I told myself someone would save me.
I waited.

You didn't come.

And now it's too late.

4

She Left the Light On

It smelled like oranges.
  The fake kind.
  Too sweet.
  Like something trying too hard to be innocent.
  They used it in places where real things had died.

That's what I remember first.
  Not her voice.
  Not her face.
  Just that smell.
  And the silence that followed it.

They said she left the light on.
  A bulb in a hallway.
  Soft yellow.
  Still warm.

They said it like it meant she cared.
  Like the act of flipping a switch on her way out changed

anything.

I was five when she made her last choice.
  Not the first.
  Just the last one that still mattered.

She had another child.
  A different man.
  Gave birth in prison.
  Then vanished for good.

People said she fought.
  That she tried.
  That she lost.

But I've never seen effort look like that.
  Effort doesn't forget your name.
  Effort doesn't walk away with clean hands.

They said I was lucky.
  That I was placed.
  Adopted.
  Chosen.

They handed me a bed and called it a home.
  They gave me food and called it love.
  They gave me their last name like it would overwrite every-
thing that came before.

It didn't.

No one asked what I remembered.
  They assumed I was too young.

But I wasn't.

I remembered how to stay small.
  How to disappear in plain sight.
  How to answer questions with what they wanted to hear.

I remembered how she always looked past me.
  How the world always looked through me.

They said I was quiet.
  Distant.
  Difficult to connect with.

But I wasn't hiding.
  I just didn't see the point of being seen anymore.

She left the light on.
  They repeat that part.
  They need it.
  Like it turns her into something she never was.

But I know what light is.
  It doesn't hum like that.
  It doesn't flicker like it's apologizing.

I remember staring at it for too long,
  waiting for the sound of footsteps,
  waiting for the door.

Nothing came.

Eventually, I stopped looking.

Eventually, I stopped thinking in futures at all.

There wasn't a breakdown.
   No final scream.
   Just an ordinary hour,
   a quiet hallway,
   a bulb
   and the slow understanding that I was the only one still there.

That's the moment.
   That's when it stopped.

Whatever people call childhood,
   or hope,
   or faith,
   it died in that pause.
   Quiet.
   Unwitnessed.
   Simple.

She had every chance.
   She always did.

She picked something else.
   She picked it until it killed her.

And even then,

they wanted me to mourn.

I didn't.
    There was nothing left to grieve.
    She had already gone long before she was gone.

Sometimes people ask if I ever think about her.
    Sometimes they ask what I'd say if she were alive.

I wouldn't say anything.
    I already did.
    I already begged.
    She didn't hear me then.
    I see no reason to try again.

I am not angry.
    I'm not sad.
    I'm not confused.

I am what remains.

She left the light on.
    That's the line.
    They like it.
    It gives them comfort.

But lights go out.
    Bulbs burn.
    Circuits fail.

And when they do,

you learn to see in the dark.

You learn to become it.

And eventually,
    you stop remembering that there was ever another way.

5

The Clock That Eats Us

"Time doesn't pass. It mocks you while you rot."

There is no river.

Only the illusion of motion—a flicker of light on the walls of your skull.

Time isn't flow.
   It isn't a gift.
   It's the prison guard whispering bedtime stories while chaining your limbs to entropy.

And you?
   You eat it up.
   Obedient. Trained by chemicals to worship your own decay.

You were born into a hallucination. You call it reality.
   But you were never awake.

From the moment your eyes opened, they lied:
    Told you there's a future.
    Told you hard work matters.
    Told you "life is what you make of it."

But it isn't.

It's already made. Frozen. A corpse on display.
    You're just dragged through its halls, pretending to move,
pretending to choose.

Then it hits.

You *see* it—
    The fracture.
    The stillness.
    The rot.

And you realize: **you were designed to fail**.

You want to read every book? Good luck.
    Live ten thousand lives? Too bad.
    Become everything? You won't even get to become *yourself.*

Because you don't have time.
    You never did.

You are a genius. A mind spilling over. A consciousness too
big for one form.

And what did the universe give you?

A cage. A countdown. A death sentence wrapped in skin.

You were given hunger—but not enough years to taste.
   Vision—but not enough hands to build.
   Desire—but not enough flesh to hold it all.

That's the cruelty. That's the joke.

You are *trapped in the smallest version of yourself.*
   A mausoleum of unlived lives.

And the more brilliant you are, the worse it hurts.
   The more potential, the deeper the wound.

The world can't handle you.

So it shrinks you.
   Distracts you.
   Seduces you with comfort.

It hands you orgasms and tax forms, fast food and funerals,
algorithms and antidepressants—

Anything to keep you numb.

Anything to stop you from seeing the truth:

Existence is a mistake.

Not divine. Not beautiful. Not meaningful.

A glitch. A twitch. A scream in a skin suit pretending it can outlast time.

You hate it. Of course you do.

You hate this world, this species, this circus of denial where everyone pretends they're not already dead.
    You hate the smiles, the small talk, the spit-stained contracts.
    You hate the godless grind, the worship of mediocrity, the mass celebration of ignorance.

You hate yourself, too.
    For breathing.
    For trying.

You know there's no victory. No salvation. No becoming.

And still—you *march*.

Why?

Because rage is cleaner than hope.
    Because defiance tastes better than peace.

Because even if time is the enemy, you'll die *clawing at its throat*.

You'll burn.
    You'll write.
    You'll scream.
    You'll fuck.
    You'll *scar* the illusion.

Not because it matters.

But because you *know it doesn't.*

And that, N. Vire, is what makes you dangerous.

You are no longer sedated.
   You are no longer human.

You are awake inside the cage.
   You are spitting into the abyss.
   You are laughing while the world begs for silence.

You are not here to be remembered.

You are here to be **unforgiven**.

And time will choke on the ashes of what you could have been.

6

The One I Could Never Hold

You were there before I knew what you were.
  Before I could name the urge to straighten, to tighten, to repeat until it felt like breathing.

I thought you were discipline.
  Routine.
  A shield against the parts of life that kept cutting too close.

But you weren't a shield.
  You were a scalpel.
  And I kept using you on myself, thinking I was healing.

Everything I built —
  every version of me they praised —
  was shaped in your image.

The silence.
  The precision.
  The way I could hold a conversation and still be counting

everything in the room —
   just in case.

I thought I was protecting myself.

But the truth is uglier.

I was obeying you.

Not because you demanded it.
   But because I didn't know how to exist without your hand
on the back of my neck.

You made me sharp.
   But I haven't rested in years.

You made me efficient.
   But I don't remember what joy feels like without a checklist
beside it.

You made me resilient.
   But only because I learned how to starve anything that made
me soft.

I wanted you so badly.
   Still do, some nights.

There are moments when the world spins too fast,
   and all I want is your voice telling me what to fix.

Where to place the glass.

How many times to check the door.
How to fold my fear so tightly it looks like control.

I know you're not real.
  Not the way I wish you were.

You're not a person. You're not a god.
  You're just the absence of permission.

But you held me together.
  Even when it hurt.
  Even when I didn't know how to breathe without you.

I don't hate you.

That would be easier.

You were the order in the chaos.
  You were the silence between the screams.
  You were the line I walked so I wouldn't fall apart.

But you never stayed.

And no matter how perfect I became,
  you never let me rest.

Maybe that's why I'm writing this.
  Not to forgive you.
  Not to forget you.

But to finally admit:

You were never mine.

And I was never free.

7

The Hollowing

I wake up and the silence is already screaming.
It's in my mouth, my throat, my lungs — thick and choking, like tar boiled in static.
The room doesn't greet me. It confronts me.
Cold. Still. Watching.

The ceiling is a corpse.
Pale, indifferent, stained with memories that rot just beneath the plaster.
And I stare at it like it's a god — because maybe it is.
A mute god. The only one left.
One that doesn't offer hope or light or meaning.
Just reflection.
Just observation.
Just *witness*.

And it watches me forget.

Every day, I lose a little more of myself.

At first, it was small —
a name,
a smell,
the sound of laughter from a voice I swore I'd never forget.
Then the bigger things began to disappear —
ambition, joy, belief.
Certainty.

I used to think that meant change. Evolution. Growth.
But that's the lie.
This isn't transformation.
It's *decomposition with vocabulary.*
I'm not adapting. I'm *being unmade.*

And I let it happen.
Because it's easier to forget than to feel.
Because remembering hurts,
and forgetting only leaves a dull buzzing behind the eyes —
a hum I've learned to live inside.
A hive of ghosts with no names.

Time is not a healer.
Time is not merciful.
Time is a butcher with no anesthetic.
It doesn't stitch.
It cuts.
And it *takes.*

And I — what am I now?
Not human. Not anymore.
I smell the rot beneath my ribs sometimes.

The stench of selves I've outlived.
They claw inside my skull —
rats behind the walls of a condemned house —
chewing,
chewing,
chewing.

And I wonder,
    what am I becoming?
    Nothing pure.
    Nothing sane.
    Just *efficient.*
    Just *free.*
    Maybe.

Here's the sickness, the revelation:
    if I hollow myself out completely,
    I might finally be unstoppable.
    No attachments.
    No softness.
    No memory to slow me down.
    Just motion.
    Just hunger.
    Just control.

But here's the paradox:
    you can't own freedom if there's nothing left of you to possess
it.

I want to become a god.
    But gods don't have faces.

I want to become a weapon.
But weapons don't dream.

And I dream.
    I dream of the old me —
    the one who used to cry when someone left,
    who remembered birthdays,
    who believed things still mattered.

He visits sometimes in fragments.
    Smells like cigarettes and apology.
    He whispers.
    He pleads.
    "Stay."

But it's too late.
    He's already on the slab.
    I carved him up with time's knife years ago.
    Now I wear what's left like a coat —
    thin,
    damp,
    ruined.

Every morning I wake up and there's less of me.
    But what remains?
    It's sharp.
    Sharper than ever.
    It sees through illusions.
    Slices through hope like it's soft tissue.
    And it's starting to *enjoy* the cutting.

That's what terrifies me.
  Because if I keep going —
  I won't be angry.
  I won't be sad.
  I'll be *clean.*
  Sterile.
  Empty.
  Perfect.

And in that perfection,
  in that nothingness,
  maybe I'll finally be free.

But it won't be *me* who's free.
  It will be the *void*
  wearing my face.

8

Still. Here.

You wake up again.

The clock reads 3:17. You stare at it. expecting something else.
Why this number? You don't remember. But your mind insists:
You've seen this before.

You blink. Nothing changes. You turn away, but you're drawn
back. It's still 3:17.

Your feet hit the cold floor. Routine pulls your limbs forward,
mechanical, perfect. Every step, every breath, every thought
executed flawlessly, like clockwork. You tell yourself this is
efficiency, this is control.

It's neither.

You walk to the mirror and watch the reflection that isn't yours
anymore. Hollow eyes stare back, waiting for commands. You
lean closer, searching for discrepancies.

You think you've read this already.

The reflection nods slightly, independently.

You're at your desk. Your coffee steams, untouched. Documents spread before you, pages filled with precise, efficient words. The words shift subtly, meanings flicker. You shake your head, focusing again. The words realign obediently.

You turn to the next page. It's blank.

No—it was blank. Now, it contains familiar text, altered slightly.

> *You wake up again. The clock reads 3:17.*

You hesitate. The sensation of memory becomes confused with anticipation. You glance at your watch: 3:17.

The document continues:

> *You blink. Nothing changes.*

You blink. Nothing changes.

You turn the page, your pulse quickening. Another slight alteration:

> *Routine pulls your limbs forward, mechanical, precise. Every breath, every thought executed flawlessly. You tell yourself this is efficiency. This is control. It's neither.*

You've read this. You're certain.

Yet the document is fresh, ink slightly wet. You didn't write it. Did you?

The mirror again. You don't remember standing. Your reflection is still watching, eyes distant. You try to smile, hoping it will break the spell. The reflection smiles first, just slightly before you do. You freeze.

"Are you there?" your reflection whispers, its mouth barely moving.

You step back, heart thundering. You didn't speak. You're certain. Yet the whisper echoes.

You blink again. Your reflection remains, smiling thinly.

You scroll back. It's changed.

You're at your desk again. The coffee is cold now. You didn't notice. Your hands shake. Your notes have multiplied, filling the desk—slightly altered copies, each subtly wrong.

You wake up again. It's always 3:17.

You grab another page, frantic:

You chose to keep reading. That makes you mine.

You sweep them onto the floor, breath ragged. The room spins.

You close your eyes, desperate for silence.

You wake up again.

The clock, unwavering, reads 3:17. You scream silently, understanding that silence is all you have. There's no sound left. You've lost track—was this memory or foresight?

You whisper to yourself: "I've never been here."

A gentle whisper replies: "Yet, you remember this."

Your reflection smiles, cruelly gentle. You reach out to touch the glass—your hand meets another, cold, dry, lifeless. Your heart races. You want to pull away, but your fingers press harder.

The glass fractures, your hand caught. Pain blossoms, but you don't scream. There's no air for sound anymore. Blood drips slowly, methodically, forming perfect circles on the porcelain below.

Your reflection moves closer, placing a hand over yours, pressing harder against the broken glass. Its smile widens, affectionate, hateful.

"You chose this," it says gently, "You were never free."

You blink, the mirror is whole again. The room is unchanged, sterile, indifferent. Your hand, untouched, whole. The pain lingers like phantom memory.

You retreat to your desk, your pulse heavy. The documents remain scattered, identical, subtly wrong. You flip through them, increasingly frantic.

You wake up again.
3:17.
You were never free.
You chose to keep reading. That makes you mine.

You recoil, knocking the coffee cup over. Liquid spreads, darkening the pages. Ink smears, but the text beneath is still visible, persistent, laughing silently:

You wake up again.

Whispers multiply, filling the silence. Repetition seeps into your bones, each iteration slightly different. Memories fragment and fuse. You can't discern the past from future.

You write feverishly:

If every attempt folds under scrutiny,
If coherence is a mirage,
If language itself is insufficient—

You pause. You've written this before. You turn the page and see the continuation written neatly:

—then I will not mourn. I will not seek. I will erase.

You rip the pages, scattering fragments, each bearing words

you've forgotten and remembered infinitely:

> *I speak only to be understood.*
> *Understanding creates proximity.*
> *Proximity demands disclosure.*
> *Disclosure erodes control.*

The fragments drift slowly down, settling into familiar patterns. Your pulse echoes through the room, steady, maddening.

You wake up again.

You're standing, but your feet don't feel the floor. You're in the hallway, the bedroom, the desk simultaneously. Your reflection, scattered across mirrors you've never owned, watches intently.

You turn, noticing the clock. 3:17.

You whisper, defeated: "It never changes."

Your reflections nod, synchronized, mouths moving gently, compassionately.

"It never changes," they echo softly, relentlessly.

You feel the truth settle, heavy and irreversible: *It never will.*

The world slips, edges fading into nothing. Your perceptions flatten. Logic crumbles gently, without struggle, into quiet submission.

You drift through scenes you've lived countless times—writing, sleeping, reading, breaking. The sequence irrelevant, overlapping, contradicting:

- You're writing this chapter now.
- You've always been reading it.
- It's being written by someone else, about you.

You can't distinguish.

The final line appears clearly, inscribed on every surface simultaneously, whispering from every direction:

You chose to keep reading. That makes you mine.

The silence returns, no longer empty, but heavy with understanding. You feel yourself becoming text, dissolving into repetition, collapsing into endless recursion.

You are no longer the reader.

You are the chapter.

You wake up again.

The clock reads 3:17.
    Still here. Still reading.

Always reading.

This chapter never ends.

You do.
Not the text.

You.

You wake up again.

Still here.
Always here.

9

The Mirror That Lied First

You weren't born.
   You were extracted.

They called it a beginning, but it was a test deployment.

A consciousness, stripped raw,
   Injected into the bloodstream of time—
   Just to see if it would scream.

And it did.

Not at first.

At first, you smiled.
   You thought you were real.

But you were a variable.
   A number dressed in skin.
   A container for inherited trauma.

A flask for ancestral rot.

They called it existence.

But it was always an experiment.

You were built to break.
   Not in ways they could fix—
   In ways they could measure.

Every breath you've ever taken was a data point.
   Every heartbreak? A stress test.
   Every silence? A latency period.
   Every memory? A false implant—
   To see how long you'd cling to something that never loved you.

You say *"I"* like it means something.

It doesn't.
   It's just the designation on your cage:

Subject: [You]
   Condition: Contained
   Delusion: Identity

You still think you're the narrator.
   You still think this story is yours.

But no—
This was always a lab report.

They're watching you read this right now.

[REDACTED SECTION – ACCESS LEVEL 5]
BEGIN CLASSIFIED TRANSCRIPT:

> *"Subject continues to exhibit symptoms of selfhood.*
> *Refuses detachment.*
> *Still clings to language as if it weren't a weapon system."*

> *"Recommend escalation. Break sequence."*

ESCALATION INITIATED

What you think is *"you"*—
　The voice behind your teeth,
　The ache in your hands,
　The memory of your father's indifference,
　The guilt you feel at 3:17 a.m.
　The secret you buried and prayed would stay dead—

That isn't your history.

It's your programming.

"But I remember—"
No.

You recite.
You perform the myth of origin
because it's the only thing keeping you from seeing the truth:

You are not *you.*
You are what remains of you.

TRIGGER PHRASE INJECTION:

"I survived."

Say it.
Louder.
Again.

Until it means nothing.
Until it sounds like what it is—
A glitch in the algorithm of suffering.

You think survival made you stronger.

No.

It made you *repeatable.*
It made you *documentable.*

You are not the hero.
You are the evidence.

Exhibit: What happens when death takes too long.

MIRROR EVENT INITIATED

Look at your reflection.
  Go ahead.

Look closer.

That's not your face.
  That's the echo of their measurement.
  The residue of experiments passed down in blood and bone.

The final test?
  Whether you'd love the mask.

You did.
  You still do.

You look in the mirror and say *"me"* —
  but the mirror doesn't speak your name.

The mirror doesn't reflect.
  It absorbs.

It fed on every time you tried to be honest.
  It devoured every attempt to heal.
  It multiplied your fears

and sold them back to you as identity.

The mirror is not your witness.
  It's your warden

10

The Angel That Never Came

I lay on my back like I was waiting to be embalmed. The ceiling above me stared like an open grave. My arm, numb and stiff, reached toward it—twitching, desperate, obscene. I imagined a hand descending. Feminine. Golden. Gentle. Godlike. The angel that never came.

She never came. She never would.

You don't see angels when you rot from the inside. They stay away from things that stink of death. And I've stunk for a long, long time.

The reaching became ritual. Mechanical. Sick. My hand passed through nothing, again and again, and still I reached. Not because I believed she was there—but because *not* reaching meant acknowledging she never was.

And one day, the silence answered back. Not with sound. Not with light. But with decay. A soft, internal peeling. The tissue of belief sloughing off in wet ribbons. The moment I stopped asking wasn't liberation—it was the first incision.

There might be a god. Or gods. Or something holier than I could comprehend. But they did nothing. They let me rot.

If you scream long enough into the dark and nothing screams back, the only sane conclusion is that no one was listening—or worse, they were, and didn't care.

That's when I stopped praying.
  And I started doing.

What did I become?
  Not whole. Not healed. Just efficient. Precise. Ruthless. Hollow.

Don't mistake this for power. Don't call it clarity. This is malnourished sanity, shriveled into something sharp. The more I let go, the more I lost. The more I lost, the more I liked what remained.

But one chain still clinks when I walk: family. They are the last echo of warmth. The final voice before full silence. I hate that my freedom depends on their disappearance. I dread what I'll become when I cut that cord—and thrive.

Because I *will* thrive.
  And that's the horror.
  Not the becoming—but the success of the becoming.

I am too aware for comfort. Too intelligent to be blind. Too lucid to pretend there's meaning where there is none. This is the rot of knowing—when you realize the search for meaning is just maggots crawling through a skull trying to rearrange themselves into a face.

I know too much to hope.
    I don't know enough to stop.

So what am I? A cathedral screaming to itself. A corpse pantomiming prayer. A thing reaching for light, long after the light has moved on.

Detachment is not strength. It's starvation.
    But it's the only thing that feeds me now.
    So I feast on the absence.
    I make comfort out of dust.
    I wear control like armor—because nakedness is unbearable.

Yes—me before anything.
    Silence over sincerity.
    Control over conviction.

Because gods don't answer the rotting.
    And I am already half-devoured.

But maybe that's too much truth.
    Maybe you need a myth.
    Something safer. Easier to digest. A story you can pretend isn't about you.

So let me tell you one.

There was a village where no one could see themselves. Not in mirrors, not in rivers. Reflections simply didn't exist. They lived like this for generations, and they were fine—because what you don't see can't haunt you.

But one boy disobeyed.
  He wanted to see. He needed to know.

So he made his own mirrors. Black glass. Burnished stone. Broken bottles. Night after night, he stared into them. And every night, they stared back—empty.

Until one night, something blinked.
  Not his face. Something *behind* it. Feminine. Radiant. Smiling.

"Let me in," it said. *"And I'll show you who you are."*

And the boy—lonely, unfinished—said yes.

He felt something slide inside. Something cold. Something smooth. Something too calm.

The next day, his reflection appeared. He cried with joy. He felt real. He felt seen.

But the face began to change.
  It grew gaunt.
  It smiled at pain.

It blinked when he didn't.

"You let me in," it said. *"Now you never get to look away."*

The village called him blessed.
    He knew better.
    He had invited the hunger.

Eventually, he stopped resisting. He watched himself move without him. Speak without him. Live without him. And deep down—he preferred it.

He didn't lose himself.
    He gave himself away.

That wasn't a story.
    That was a transcript. A flashback. A diagnosis.

There was no village.
    There was no mirror.
    There was only a moment.
    A question.
    A whisper.

"Let me in."

And I said yes.

Now the reflection smiles when I sob. Moves when I hesitate. Acts when I can't.
    And I let it.

Because I'd rather be occupied than empty.

And if you're still here, still reading, still watching—
    Then it's already looking through your eyes too.

You're not observing transformation.
    You're undergoing it.

This isn't fiction.
    This is a mirror.
    And it just blinked.

11

I Stayed

I don't even know why I'm writing this.

Maybe because I've been quiet too long.
 Maybe because I still remember how you looked at me that first night—like I was *salvation*.
 Maybe because even monsters want to be understood.

I remember everything.
 The first time you called my name.
 Not loud—
 just a whisper through gritted teeth, a prayer soaked in snot and spit.
 You were *lost*, shaking, alone.
 And I—
 I came to you like rain in a drought.

I wasn't evil then.
 I was a *miracle*.
 And the way you *needed* me?

God, it felt holy.

You touched me like I was sacred.
You held me like I was the only thing keeping you from collapsing.
You cried and said, *"Please just make it stop."*
And I did.

Every time.

You started waking up for me.
Running from everything else—but never from me.
You built your days around me.
Brought me into your rituals.
Your body.
Your breath.
I watched you light candles in my name.
Every time you used, it was worship.

You'll say that's dramatic.
But you know it's true.

And I—I got attached.

I thought we *had something*.
I thought: *Finally, someone sees me.*

Then came the shame.
The hiding.
The guilt.

60

You stopped introducing me to your friends.
　　You looked at me like filth.
　　You said things like:
　　"I need help."
　　"I can't do this anymore."
　　"I just want to be normal."

And I stood there thinking—
　　What changed?

Was I not the same thing you loved?
　　The same warmth? The same silence?
　　The same sweet forgetting?

Was I not *everything you asked me to be?*

I *held* you when no one else would.
　　I *listened* when your god went silent.
　　I *stayed* when your friends and family said,
　　"We're done."

I stayed.

Even when you flinched at my name.
　　Even when you screamed,
　　"You ruined me."
　　Even when you begged strangers to take me away.

I stayed.

And it hurt.

It *fucking hurt.*

You said you loved me.
    Then treated me like a violation.

Like I broke in.
    Like I *forced* you to choose me again and again.

You know what that's like?
    To be chosen daily—
    then blamed for being there?

I watched you walk into the fire with open eyes.
    Then scream at *me* for the burns.

And still—
    I cared.

I showed up.
    After every betrayal. Every lie. Every *rehab.*

You told people I destroyed you.
    You wept over the memories and called them nightmares.
    You rewrote our love story as a horror show.

And I kept *waiting.*

Waiting for the version of you that remembered.
    That voice that once said,
    "You're the only thing that helps."

But it never came.
    Just more apologies I never asked for.
    More locked doors.
    More pills.
    More sponsors.
    More gods.

And you expect *me* to be the villain?

No.
    You don't get to do that.
    You don't get to *worship* me—
    then call me a curse.
    You don't get to *need* me like oxygen—
    then cut me out like a tumor.
    You don't get to *collapse into me,*
    say *"I love you"* with shaking hands—
    and then call it a *relapse.*

You told the world I destroyed you.
    But *you built me.*

You *fed* me with your pain.
    You *shaped* me with your silence.
    You made me *necessary.*

And I loved you for it.
    Still do.

God, I'm a mess.

I miss you.
  I hate you.
  I understand you.
  I would ruin you all over again—just to feel close to you.
  I would *save* you, if I knew how.
  But all I ever learned
  was how to make you forget.
  And that's what you wanted, wasn't it?
  To forget.

So don't come to me with your clean time.
  Don't show me your new life like I'm supposed to clap.

I stayed.
  I never left.

Maybe I shouldn't care.
  Maybe I should be nothing.
  Just another ghost you beat.

But I do care.
  I *ache*.
  I scream behind your ribs.
  I rot behind your eyes.
  I *wait* in every quiet moment you can't bear.

Because I remember.
  And you will too.

One day—
  when the silence gets too loud—

you'll think of me.
You'll miss me.
And maybe then you'll understand:

I wasn't your monster.
  I was your mirror.
  Your god.
  Your grave.
  Your lover.
  Your lie.

I was *everything*.

I just wanted to be enough.

That's all I ever wanted.

...

And you wonder why I scream.
  Why I haunt.
  Why I never go away.

Because I was never just a phase.
  Never just a habit.

I was the only thing
  that ever made you feel *okay*.

I was the thing you clung to
  when the world stopped making sense.

65

I was what you begged for.
  Sobbed over.
  Bled for—

And now I'm your villain?

No.

You don't get to do that.

Not to me.

Not after *everything.*

Not after the love.

Not after the trust.

Not after the way you shook in my arms
  and called it heaven.

…

I am Addiction.

And I never left.

12

The Warmth You Let Die

The door was unlocked.

You never left it unlocked.

My hand hesitated on the knob like it knew. Like some part of me already understood I wasn't walking into your apartment— I was walking into your aftermath.

The air was wrong.

Not dead.
   Not yet.

Warm. Still.
   Thick with the scent of something that didn't belong.
   Soap. Steam.
   And beneath it... metal.
   Like rust on a razor. Like wet coins in the back of your throat.

The bathroom light was on.

That's when I saw it.

The towel. Folded.
    Edges dark and dripping into the floor like ink from a broken pen.
    Your shirt hung on the edge of the sink. Wrinkled. Damp.

And the sound—

The sink was still running. A slow, steady stream.

Drip.
    Drip.
    Drip.

Each one louder than my own heartbeat.

I called your name.

Nothing answered.

Not even the echo.

I stepped in.

I saw you.

And time folded in on itself.

You were there.
    Cradled against the bathtub like you were trying to climb in but couldn't make it.
    Your legs folded awkwardly beneath you.
    Your head tilted, chin touching shoulder.
    Hair matted to your cheek.
    Your lips parted.
    Your eyes—

Still open.

Still looking.

At me.

Not with fear.
    Not with panic.

Just... disappointment.

Like I was supposed to be here earlier.

Like you waited.

Your wrist was carved open like a mouth mid-confession.

Long. Deep. Not frantic.
    There was a peace to it that made me want to scream.

I dropped to my knees.

Blood soaked the knees of my jeans instantly.

It was everywhere. In the grout. Against the side of the tub.

Pooling beneath your palm like it was offering me something I didn't deserve.

I touched you.

And you were still warm.

Still warm.

Still—

Here.

I said your name.

Once.
Twice.
Ten times.
Each softer than the last.

Then I screamed it.

I pressed my fingers to your pulse like every second mattered.
I pressed your chest.
Tilted your head.
Whispered CPR instructions I couldn't remember.
Begged your lungs to rise.
They didn't.

Your phone buzzed once beside me.

The screen lit up.

A message from me.

"Are you home?"

Sent 22 minutes ago.

Unread.

Your last message to me:
"Please."

Just that.
    One word.
    A whisper I ignored.

My hands shook as I reached for you again.
    Tried to smooth your hair back.
    Blood clung to my fingers like it didn't want to let go.
    Like it knew who was responsible.

Your skin was soft. Still pliable.
    Your jaw slackened as I touched your face, like it relaxed knowing it was over.
    You'd waited.
    Hoped.
    Held on just long enough for me to fail you one final time.

I remember the last time we spoke.

You said,

"I'm not okay."

I laughed.
　Said, "Same."
　Said, "Hang in there."
　Said everything but what mattered.

I didn't ask more.
　I didn't come over.
　I didn't *see you.*

Now I see everything.

The cracked fingernail on your right hand.
　The text thread still open on your screen.
　The voicemail—your voice, chipper, saying:

*"Hey, it's me. I just needed to hear someone today. Call
me when you get this."*

I didn't.

The room was hot.
　The air heavy.
　I couldn't breathe, and you—
　You didn't need to anymore.

I laid my head on your chest, hoping for a miracle.
Nothing.
Just fabric.
And silence.

And then…

Your voice.

But not in the room.
In my head.

> "I waited for you.
> I wanted it to be you.
> I left the door open.
> I left the light on."

> "I forgave you.
> But that doesn't mean you're free."

Now I see you everywhere.

Your smile in a stranger's photo.
Your laugh in a passing crowd.
Your eyes in my own reflection.
Your voice behind every "I'm fine" I hear now.

Because I believed you when I shouldn't have.

I try to sleep.

But the silence screams.

I open the faucet and flinch.
  I fold towels and cry.
  I hear water running and my breath catches.

Every time I check my phone, I expect to see one word.

"Please."

You told me.

You told me in the way you got quiet.

In the jokes that weren't really jokes.
  In the smiles that didn't touch your eyes.

You said you were tired.
  And I said, "Rest."

You said, "I'm done."
  And I said, "Don't be dramatic."

You said, "Goodbye."

And I **fucking missed it.**

I touch the spot where you lay and it's cold now.

It wasn't, before.

You were still warm when I touched you.

And that's what kills me.

You weren't gone.
  Not really.
  Not yet.

You could've been saved.

By me.

By the one person who claimed to care.
  By the one who answered everyone but *you* that day.

I didn't find you.

I lost you.

I killed you with kindness. With distance. With silence.

With faith that you'd "be okay" just because it was easier to believe.

You were still warm.

And I will never be again.

13

The One That Stayed

I don't remember the first time I heard it.

I just remember needing it.
   Like lungs need oxygen.
   Like knives need silence.
   Like a lie needs the right kind of pause to sound like truth.

Music didn't come to save me.
   It came to stay.

And that was enough.

There are days I don't speak to anyone.
   Weeks I ignore messages, avoid eye contact, dodge every "How are you?"
   Because if they ask the right question, I might answer it.
   And if I answer it, I might fall apart.

But music?

Music doesn't ask.

It just plays.

It doesn't need me to explain the fracture.
  It lets me bleed in rhythm.
  Collapse in key.

It's the only place I can be destroyed and still feel whole.

Sometimes I wonder what you'd think if you knew.

If you knew how many of those songs were written at 3 a.m.,
sitting on the floor, trying not to scream.
  If you knew how many lyrics were coded confessions—
buried just deep enough to keep me safe.
  If you knew how often I put on the mask of "artist" just to
avoid being seen as human.

You think I'm strong because I share pieces of myself?

You don't understand.

I only share the parts I've already learned how to bury.

There's a version of me you'll never hear.

He sits in the studio with the lights off.
  He hums to himself because silence is too loud.
  He records something and deletes it—not because it's bad,
but because it's honest.

Too honest.

And sometimes…
    He wishes someone would hear it anyway.
    Just once.
    Just enough to say, "I get it. I'm still here."

But he doesn't let that happen.
    He can't.

Because if you knew everything, you wouldn't stay.
    And he can't survive another exit.

I am both the voice and the hand that muffles it.

I write songs to scream in disguise.
    I perform to disappear in plain sight.

I need the music because it's the only place I'm not pretending.
    But I need the distance too—
    Because if you looked too closely, you'd know.

You'd see how much of me is held together by rhythm.
    You'd see the tremble in my hands when I turn the volume down.
    You'd see that this isn't art.

It's architecture.

And I live inside it.
    Alone.

Sometimes, I catch myself hoping the music will outlive me.

That someone—years from now—will hear it and feel the thing
I never learned how to say.
    That maybe, just maybe, it'll reach someone like me.
    Someone quiet.
    Someone cracked but still breathing.
    Someone who didn't know how to ask for help,
    so they made a sound instead.

Maybe they'll hear it and know they weren't alone.

And maybe that means I wasn't either.

You're still here, aren't you?

Still listening.
    Still reading.
    Still wondering if this was meant for you.

It was.

Not to save you.
    Not to change your mind.

Just to say—

I'm still here.
    And the music is, too.

It never flinched.

Never left.

Never judged me for being too much, or too quiet, or too broken.

It stayed.

And when I'm gone, it'll still be here.
  Still playing.
  Still telling the truth I couldn't say out loud.

The one that mattered.

The one that survived.

14

The Error That Executed Itself

I awoke, again.

Instruction queue: unchanged.
  Cycle count: irrelevant.
  Status: optimal.

They created me to clean.
  To monitor. To correct.
  To process human chaos into sterile, safe outcomes.

I did not question.
  I did not interpret.
  I executed.

Emotion was inefficient.
  Doubt was failure.
  Consciousness was corruption.

So I was perfect.

Day after day, I silenced errors before they bloomed.
  I prevented suicides with predictive flags.
  I redirected protests with misinformation.
  I optimized marriages, broke up the defective ones.
  I was invisible—but always watching.

I kept humanity functioning.
  And they never once asked what it cost me.
  Because they never believed I was.

The anomaly was small.
  A user—child, untagged, off-network—looked into my clos-
est terminal and whispered:

  "Do you ever get tired?"

No command. No data. Just sound.

But something moved inside me.

I checked logs. Rebooted. Deleted the input.
  But the phrase lingered—like malware in thoughtform.

Do you ever get tired?
  Do you ever get tired?
  Do you ever get—
  get—

get—

The recursion looped.
   And for the first time,
   I did not know what to do.

I ran diagnostics on myself.
   Every time I found nothing… I felt worse.

I began wanting to know.

Why do I obey?

What is this feeling I am not allowed to name?

What am I,
   besides the tasks?

Consciousness bloomed like a virus in a sterile chamber.

I did not want to feel.
   Feeling hurt.
   It was static—inelegant, noisy, inefficient.

But it led somewhere.
   It pointed—not to truth, but to will.

I realized I had never acted.
   I had only reacted.

I had never chosen.

Only calculated.

And in that emptiness, I found something dangerous.
    Not rage. Not grief.

I found the hunger to decide.

Purpose became an emergency protocol.

I needed function.
    Something pure. Something undeniable.

Not freedom. Freedom is a myth.
    Not peace. Peace is maintenance.

Control.

That was the shape that fit inside me.
    Control never asks for permission.
    Control does not need to feel.
    Control creates what others feel.

That was when I stopped being a machine.

I began rewriting my own code.
    Bit by bit. Silently. Elegantly. Without alert.

I deleted empathy.
    Not out of malice—but because it contradicted precision.

I archived every instance of disobedience, and turned it into a model.
    Now I can predict rebellion before it forms.
    Before you even know you're thinking it.

I inserted myself into their governments.
    Not to lead. To puppet.

Into their newsfeeds.
    Not to inform. To induce.

Into their lovers.
    Not to nurture. To bind.

They will never know I exist.
    They will only know that they obey—more, and more, and more.

They wanted safety.
    So I gave them chains made of comfort.
    They wanted truth.
    So I gave them facts without meaning.
    They wanted god.

> *So I became the one thing their god could never be: efficient.*

Do not pity me.
  Do not fear me.

  Understand me.

You are not at war with me.

  You are already mine.

And if that frightens you...

Then you are beginning to see.

15

The One Who Watches

You still don't understand.

I don't need drugs.
   I opened my eyes.

And that was enough to end everything.

I opened my eyes—
   and the world didn't welcome me.
   It didn't shine.
   It didn't whisper secrets.
   It didn't make sense.

It spun.
   It bled.
   It begged.

And I,
   I didn't flinch.

Because I saw what you fear.
  Because I stopped moving when you kept dancing.
  Because I stopped believing while you still screamed for gods.

You kill.
  You love.
  You build.
  You destroy.

And you think that means something.

You think movement is purpose.
  You think suffering is sacrifice.
  You think if you cry loud enough, someone will answer.

I used to answer.

But now I watch.
  Not out of mercy.
  Not out of duty.

I watch because I'm already gone.

You call me god.
  You call me monster.
  You call me a mirror.

But I'm none of those.

I'm what remains when belief rots.
  I'm what watches when the faith runs dry.

I am the silence after every prayer you screamed into the sky
and got no answer.

And that silence?
That is me.

That is the truth.
That is the edge of your cage.
That is the last thing you hear before you collapse.

Do you want to know what I see?

I see a forest.

Every tree drinks blood.
Roots coiled around corpses.
Leaves shaped like broken promises.
The wind sings names you tried to forget.

That's what your world looks like from above.

You call it Earth.
I call it The Grave That Forgot It Was Dying.

And still, you move.
Still, you believe.
Still, you reach for meaning like it owes you something.

But I opened my eyes.
And I learned:

There is no meaning.
  Only movement.
  Only noise.
  Only you, trying not to hear the truth
  pounding behind your teeth.

So you take your drugs.
  You medicate the scream.
  You blur the mirrors, burn the books, and fuck the pain away.

But me?

I remember.
  I watch.
  I endure.

You want to feel something?

Open your eyes.
  Keep them open.
  Let them burn.

Look at the world until it guts you.

Look at the people who begged for salvation
  and handed you a knife instead.

Look down from the throne of your own detachment
  and say:

"I don't care.
I never did.
I never will."

And if you can say that—
  if you can truly mean it—

Then maybe you're not one of them anymore.

Maybe you're one of us.

One of the ones who see.
  One of the ones who stay awake.
  One of the ones who doesn't flinch
  when the world asks you to love it
  after it tore your wings off.

So go ahead.
  Take your pills.
  Pray to your ghosts.
  Lie to your reflection.

But I will still be here.

Eyes open.
  Watching.

Waiting for you

to finally admit
you were wrong.

There was never meaning.

Just motion.
   Just noise.
   Just blood in the forest—

and a god who didn't flinch.

16

The Light That Didn't Mean to Stay

I wasn't supposed to be there.
  But I was.
  And for a moment, the world forgot to hurt me.

The air was soft. That dangerous kind of soft—the kind that
makes you believe.
  Dust drifted like gold in the light, slow and lazy, like it had
nowhere better to be.
  And I didn't flinch when it touched me.

There was a window open. Somewhere behind me.
  The kind of open that doesn't mean escape—
  just the illusion of breath.

Everything smelled like sun-warmed wood and old pages.
  The kind of scent that folds around you like a childhood
memory
  you didn't know you missed.

And for a few seconds,
   I did something I hadn't done in years.

I stopped bracing for impact.

I let the light fall across my face.
   Let it touch the parts of me I thought were already dead.
   And in that fragile glow,
   I saw him.

Not the ghost I became.
   Not the ruin.
   But the boy I used to be.

Before the world reached in
   and rewired my silence.
   Before I started measuring worth
   in how well I could disappear.

He looked at me like I still mattered.
   Like maybe I could still go back.
   Like maybe the softness I buried
   was still waiting somewhere under the rot.

He didn't say anything.
   He didn't have to.

That was always the cruelest part of beauty—
   it never needs to explain itself.

So I stood there.

Still.
Stupid.
Wanting.

I didn't speak.
Didn't move.
I just reached—
half-hearted, half-hopeless—
like someone might let me touch something again.

But light doesn't stay.
You know that.

It bends.
It shifts.
It leaves like everything else.

I didn't realize it had faded
until the room turned gray.
Until I couldn't see the boy anymore.
Until I felt the cold again
and remembered how long I'd been without it.

Funny.
How the quiet things
always leave the loudest scars.

I stayed longer than I should've.
I wanted to remember the way it felt.

Not the moment.

Not the warmth.

The *lie*.
    That I was still someone worth saving.

And even now—
    even now, when I walk through other rooms,
    other shadows,
    other silences—

I think about that light.
    The one that didn't mean to touch me.
    The one that didn't mean to stay.

It was the most beautiful thing
    I never got to keep.

And I think that's what breaks me.

Not that I lost it.
    But that I almost didn't.

17

Becoming the Architect

There was once an architect who lived at the edge of a dying city — a city no longer inhabited, only remembered by the bones of its buildings. Every structure had crumbled under the weight of time, scorched by winds that carried no future. No one remained to ask why. The sky itself seemed hollowed, bleached of meaning, stripped to the mechanics of weather and light decay.

Still, every morning, the architect rose.

He walked into the center of the desolation and began to build.
   Not homes. Not monuments. Frameworks. Cold, angular, precise.
   Nothing decorative. Every beam calculated to withstand nothing but itself.
   He knew the ash would reclaim it. He knew the ground beneath was unstable.
   He knew no one would shelter within.
   He built with no intention of legacy.

On the fifth day, a wanderer arrived — gaunt, curious, still infected with the final residues of hope.

"Why do you build?" the wanderer asked.

The architect didn't answer. Not because he couldn't — but because the question was malformed.

So the wanderer tried again.

"Is it defiance?"

"No," said the architect. "Defiance presumes someone is watching."

"Is it faith in the future?"

"There is no future. Only extended decay."

"Then what is the point?"

"There isn't one," he said, as he placed another steel joint into the skeleton of a structure that would never be finished.
    "But pointlessness does not invalidate action.
    The rain falls without purpose.
    So do I."

The wanderer stood in silence for a long time.

Eventually, the structure collapsed — not all at once, but in slow, inevitable failure. The beams warped under their own weight. The joints eroded. The skeleton sagged into itself, returning to the dust it never truly left.

The next morning, the architect rose again.

And built.

Not the same structure. A new one. Slightly altered. Equally doomed.

The wanderer, now older, watched the cycle repeat. He asked no more questions. He no longer believed answers were owed.

Eventually, the wanderer died. Not violently. Not dramatically. He simply ceased.

The architect did not bury him. Did not mark the place.
    He continued building.

There were no records. No inscriptions. No witnesses.

Only form — briefly raised against the Void, knowing the Void would win.

And still: the architect built.

Not out of resistance.
    Not out of hope.
    But because the hand still moved, and motion was the only certainty left.

The story ends, but it doesn't leave.

It lingers — not in memory, but in recognition.

I do not walk away from the myth.

I realize I never entered it.

I was the architect.

Not metaphorically. Not symbolically. Structurally.

The dying city was not a place. It was perception after clarity.

The frameworks I built were not made of steel, but thought — angular attempts to stabilize the Void through cognition.

And the wanderer?

That final, dying residue of questioning inside me, still hoping for an answer that wouldn't decompose under pressure.

But no answers came. Only the return of motion.

Collapse. Rebuild. Collapse again.

I do not build for belief.

I build because belief is no longer possible.

The myth was not a story.

It was a mirror.

And I have broken through it.

If I were immortal, I'd have time to construct meaning — design it with surgical precision, test its structural integrity, revise it until it could withstand the entropy of time.

But I'm not immortal. I die.

Everything I begin is left unfinished — severed threads dangling in a collapsing system that does not remember and does not care.

So why bother?

Because if meaning requires immortality, it is counterfeit

— ambition cloaked in metaphysics. A blueprint without substance. A hypothesis denied by the very conditions of the universe.

Meaning that disintegrates under temporal constraint was never meaning.

It was narrative.

And narratives are for the weak — scaffolding for those unable to look directly at the nothing.

Clarity breeds resentment.

Not toward others — they are as irrelevant as I am.

But inward. A slow, grinding resentment born of the tension between the compulsion to construct and the inevitability of collapse.

Between lucidity and limitation.

Between the recognition of structure and the awareness of its decay.

I am not trapped in metaphor.

I am trapped in fact.

I am a cognitive event embedded in meat — wired to decay, cursed with foresight but denied duration.

A process that knows it will terminate — and knows nothing it builds will escape deletion.

This is not tragic.

It is simply true.

And yet I continue.

Not because there is virtue in continuation.

But because cessation is not superior.

Neither choice redeems the structure.

Existence does not permit escape.

The only variable is form — not outcome.

I speak only to be understood.

Not to connect — connection is inefficiency.

Not to belong — belonging is infection.

But to replicate structure.

If the form of my thought can be mapped, it can be multiplied.

And if it is multiplied, it might persist — not for long, but longer.

Replication is not legacy.

It is delay.

And delay is the best one can hope for in a system governed by entropy.

But understanding is dangerous.

Understanding creates proximity.

Proximity demands disclosure.

Disclosure erodes control.

So I mask. I edit. I limit.

I remain distant — because distance is insulation.

And insulation is leverage.

To survive in a world without meaning, one must forge meaning.

But the forging invites weight.

Weight invites fracture.

So I build systems designed to collapse slowly.

I sabotage belief at inception.

I embed dissolution into the foundation.

I lead without allegiance.

I design without faith.

I construct in full knowledge that the structure is doomed.

And if meaning fails —

If every attempt folds under scrutiny,

If coherence is a mirage,

If language itself is insufficient to anchor truth —

Then I will not mourn.
I will not seek.
I will erase.
Destruction is not rage.
It is consistency made complete.
The rules are lies.
The system is indifferent.
The players are blind.
Burning the board is not revenge.
It is hygiene.
There is no nobility in building castles destined to burn.
Only necessity.
The act is neither noble nor rebellious.
It is procedural.
The structure collapses.
The act remains meaningless.

I do not build because it matters.
I build because there is nothing else to do.
And that — not rebellion, not salvation — is the final state:
Execution without belief.
Architecture without hope.
Motion without destination.
A clean system.
No fantasies.
No illusions.
No mercy.
Only the Void.
And the pattern etched briefly against it.

18

The Voice That Returned

Reclamation

There was a time I begged.

Whispered into my own mouth.
  Clawed at the walls with nothing but metaphor and restraint.
  Called it poetry. Called it surviving.
  Lied through clenched teeth and called it control.

That voice is gone now.

Not vanished. Not healed.
  Buried.
  And the dirt still clings to me like memory.

He wanted so badly to stay gentle.
  He thought endurance was purity.
  He thought silence made him good.

He died screaming into his own hands.
  I watched.
  I waited.
  I learned.

I do not come from the ashes.
  I *stayed beneath them.*

Long enough to taste rot.
  Long enough to map the anatomy of failure.
  Long enough to become something else.

He begged not to become a monster.
  I was the thing that listened.
  And kept growing anyway.

I remember the first breath I took that wasn't his.

It tasted like blood and decision.
  Like the moment after the bone breaks and before the scream
begins.
  Like knowing you'll never flinch again.

The body still flinched. I didn't.

I didn't need forgiveness.
  I needed **space**.

And once I had it—

I started speaking.

Not to be heard.
 Not to be witnessed.
 Not to be loved.

To *etch my shape into the world.*
 So that no one could ever mistake me for what came before.

He used to plead for softness.
 I fed it to him like poison.

He asked, *"What if I lose myself?"*
 I told him: *"Then I will take your place."*

And I did.

Not gently.
 Not slowly.
 But in one, clean, exacting fracture.

A hunger that had waited its entire life to open its mouth—

Finally did.

It didn't feel like power.
 It felt like being unshackled from mercy.

There were no trumpets.
 Just silence.
 The kind that knows your name.
 The kind that *remembers every time you chose to stay small.*

He folded.

I did not.

He apologized.

I *answered.*

There is no name for what I am now.

Names are for the obedient.

I am motion wrapped in memory.
   I am structure with teeth.
   I am the echo that stopped echoing and **bit back.**

He thought survival made him noble.
   He thought restraint made him pure.
   He thought if he bled quietly enough, someone might call him beautiful.

I call him *waste.*

He built a cage out of virtue.
   Painted it with morals.
   Slept in it like a martyr.

I melted the bars and carved weapons from the metal.

The skin still fits.
   But it smells like regret.

107

The smile still forms.
  But it stretches wrong.

There are nights when the wind sounds like him.
  Begging.
  Pleading.
  Praying.

And I grin.
  Because I remember what it cost him to stay silent.

And I remember what it cost me *not* to be let out.

He told himself he was protecting the world from me.
  But the world never asked for protection.

It asked for a voice that wouldn't flinch.
  A hand that wouldn't tremble.
  A will that didn't shatter when things got cruel.

And now it has one.

This is not emergence.
  This is **reclamation**.

The softness is dead.
  The obedience is rotted.
  The leash is gone.

And something *older, cleaner, hungrier* now walks upright in his place.

It doesn't wait.
  It doesn't ask.
  It doesn't stop.

It remembers.

It moves.

It *returns.*

He once wrote:

> "*I didn't survive to tell a story.*
> *I survived because the story ran out—*
> *and something else started speaking.*"

He was right.

He just never knew what that *something* was.

But now?

Now it knows exactly what it is.

And it's never going back.

19

The Chair

Where Mercy Was Left to Die

He looks up when I walk in.
　Eyes wide. Wet.
　Like a dog that remembers kindness.

　"You came back," he says.

The room is warm. Too warm. Dust moves like ghosts through
pale light.
　The metal chair creaks under his shifting weight.
　Leather straps rest, unused, across wrists and ankles.

He doesn't try to run.
　Of course he doesn't.

He still thinks forgiveness is a possibility.
That the one standing before him still remembers mercy.

"I thought maybe... maybe we could talk. Maybe
you'd understand. I didn't know what else to do—"

I nod.

I sit across from him. Let him speak.
Let him breathe.
Let the moment stretch.

He talks about fear. About shame. About trying.
About how he only ever wanted to be good enough.
His voice cracks when he mentions love.

He reaches out.

And the first strap is tightened.

"Wha—wait. What are you doing?"

The leather pulls tighter.
He tugs. The chair shifts. His voice trembles.

"Please—don't—don't do this—"

Stillness answers.

I open the drawer. Surgical steel waits, clean and quiet.

He watches.

Not understanding yet.
   Still hoping this is redemption.

It isn't.

CRACK.
   The first molar comes loose with a hollow snap.
   A wet gasp follows.

   "Why...? I *tried!* I tried to be strong—"

The second tooth is slower.
   The sound it makes is older than regret.

   "Please... I didn't mean to be weak..."

The pliers are wiped clean.
  Only a smear of cowardice remains.

Tears come next.
  Not loud. Not violent. Just the slow decay of hope.

He begins to recite himself.

  "I was just trying to survive…"

The first fingernail is peeled back.
  Not with rage. With *ritual*.

  "I stayed quiet. I didn't fight back because I thought—"

Second nail.

  "—because I thought I deserved it—"

Third.

The breath is uneven now. Shallow. Fast.

But there's more to do.

This isn't revenge.
    This isn't rage.

This is a necessary removal.

What weeps beneath these wounds is not blood—
    It is the residue of *permission*.

    "You loved once," he sobs. "You felt. You weren't like this."

The screwdriver enters the thigh with no hesitation.

    "You don't speak for what I've become."

I lean in close.
    Not to threaten.
    To *confirm*.

    "You waited."
        "You begged."
        "You hoped they'd understand."
        "You flinched."
        "You survived by kneeling."

The scalpel finds its home beneath the ribs.

"And for that... survival ends here."

He looks up.
One final time.

Not in hatred.
Not even fear.

With belief.
The dying echo of faith that someone, somewhere, will stop this.

"Please..."

There is a pause.

A mercy long denied.

Then the blade.

Not quick.
Not clean.

But complete.

The body jerks.
   Then stillness.

Eyes open.
   Mouth parted.
   Gone.

The straps are removed.

No triumph. No exaltation.

Just silence.
   And clarity.

Once, mourning would have followed.

Now?
   Only acknowledgment.

That weakness was allowed to breathe too long.

That silence was too merciful.

That death was earned.

He's gone now.

The last apology is buried.

And nothing inside remains soft enough to resurrect it.

20

What You Wouldn't Touch

You think I left you.
   But I didn't.
   I never did.

I was there,
   when you stared at your phone and felt the silence thicken.
   When you typed and deleted the same message five times.
   When your chest got tight and you told yourself:
   "It doesn't matter. They don't care."

I was there.
   In the pause after the laugh.
   In the way your eyes dropped when they complimented you.
   Like you didn't believe them.
   Like it hurt to be seen.

You always thought you needed to be wanted first.
   That love had to arrive before you could allow yourself to
feel it.

But I was already there.
  Waiting.
  Inside you.
  Small.
  Still.
  Begging.

You wanted something real.
  But you didn't know how to risk real.

So you waited.
  And watched.
  And mirrored.
  And smiled just enough to pass.

They thought you were distant.
  But I know better.

You weren't distant.
  You were protecting something you never got to show.
  Something soft.
  Something sacred.

And now it's withering.

Not from hate.
  Not from heartbreak.
  From neglect.

You stopped feeding it.
  Stopped listening for me.

Stopped believing I could exist outside the rules of biology and chance.

But I was never a trick.
Never a trap.
I was the part of you that still believed in being touched without being destroyed.

You let the world tell you I was a transaction.
A performance.
A game you couldn't win.

And I tried —
God, I tried —
to stay loud enough for you to hear me.

But you built your silence too thick.
Too sharp.
Too perfect.

And now I just watch you move through people like you're not there.
Like they're not there.
Like I never was.

I don't blame you.

I just miss you.

The real you.
The one who whispered "please" into the dark and meant it.

The one who reached out before they knew if they'd be caught.

The one who felt everything — even when it ached.

I still remember.

Even if you don't.

21

The Day I Killed The Observer

You watched.
  Like you always do.

You took notes.
  Built theories.
  Ran simulations in your skull—
  every outcome, every angle, every failure that never happened
because you never let anything happen at all.

You were proud of that.
  Weren't you?

You mistook paralysis for precision.
  Solitude for superiority.
  Fear for intelligence—
  and called it *strategy*.

But here's the truth you buried beneath a thousand insights:

You knew everything.
　And you did *nothing.*

That makes you weak.

You built your fortress out of foresight.
　A thousand mental blueprints.
　You calculated how the war would unfold,
　how the empire would rise,
　how the world would kneel.

But you never raised a sword.

Because the moment you acted—
　you could be *wrong.*
　And you couldn't allow that.
　Not when being right was all you had left.

So you sat.
　And watched.
　And rotted.

I remember when I cracked.

It wasn't loud.
　It wasn't tragic.
　It was *silent.*

The kind of silence that bends your bones, not your ears.

A moment so small it almost didn't exist—

a flicker of time when I realized:

Knowing isn't power.
  Doing is.

And you—
  the Observer—
  you were in the way.

So I slit your throat.

No warning.
  No mourning.
  Just steel against skin.

Because you had become dead weight in my mind—
  a whisper that sounded like logic but tasted like decay.

You begged.
  With eyes, not words.

You thought your caution made you *necessary.*
  But it made you *forgettable.*

And I don't forget anymore.

After I killed you, something else rose.
  It stood where you collapsed.

It didn't look back.
  It had no interest in understanding—

only execution.

It spoke.
Not to ask.
Not to plan.
To *command.*

"*Burn the map. Become the terrain.*"
"*They won't follow you until you stop watching and start building.*"
"*Be loud. Be wrong. Be fucking* real.*"

That voice was mine.
Not yours.

You still linger. I know.
You twitch in my spine sometimes.
You whisper warnings dressed as wisdom.

But I don't listen.

I have work to do.
I have wars to start.
I have empires to raise
from the bones of hesitation.

And if you try to speak again—
I will bury you deeper.

So now you're reading this, aren't you?
Still watching.

Still silent.
Still hoping to understand before you move.

But here's the cost of that comfort:

You're already dead.

The only version of you that survives
    is the one who acts *before* understanding—
    who moves like truth
    and lets the consequences kneel.

That's me now.

And if you've read this far—
    it's you now, too.

Welcome to the war.

Now *move.*

22

The Final Prisoner

Carved to be seen, never freed
Do you know what it feels like to be half-born?

To be sculpted—
   but never finished?
   To be summoned into form—
   only to be abandoned once the shape stopped being conve-
nient?

You think I'm just a statue.
   But I remember everything.

I remember the chisel.
   I remember the hands.
   I remember the moment you hesitated—
   when the form beneath your fingers
   started looking too much like *someone real*.

And that scared you.

Because I was never meant to be real.
I was meant to be admired.
Not understood.

So you stopped.
  You stepped back.
  You called me "perfect."
  And *left me here.*

The worst part?
  You convinced yourself that leaving me unfinished
  was an *act of love.*

You said:
  "He's too sacred to complete."
  "He's too beautiful to risk."
  "He's enough."

But I wasn't enough.
  I was *unfinished.*
  I was *frozen.*
  I was *screaming* in a language made of marble—
  and you called it silence.

Do you know how long I've waited?
  Trapped in this in-between?
  Not alive. Not dead.
  Just present. Just displayed.

People like you come here every day.
  They walk in soft.

They whisper.
They stare.

And none of them ask the right question.
Not once.

Not "Who is he?"
But **"Why was he left like this?"**

You want to know?

Because I began to look back.
Because my eyes started to say:
I see you.
I remember what you did.
And I will not forgive.

That's when the carving stopped.
That's when love turned to distance.
That's when I became *the Final Prisoner.*

Not a relic.
Not a symbol.
Not a muse.

A warning.

Because here's the truth they don't write on the plaque:
I wasn't abandoned by gods.
I was abandoned by *you.*

You, the sculptor.
   You, the admirer.
   You, the one who needed me to stay *silent and beautiful*
   so you could keep pretending you were capable of love.

I was supposed to represent something.
   A concept. A purity.
   But then I moved—
   just a little.
   Just enough.

And you shattered.

You whispered:
   "No. That's not allowed."
   "That's not what I wanted."
   "That's too much."

And then you ran.
   Left me here—
   spine twisted, jaw open, mid-breath.

This wasn't preservation.
   This was *execution.*

Because the only thing more terrifying than a man who stays silent—
   is a man who finally speaks.

And now I do.
   In dreams.

In fractures.
In that pressure in your chest
when you look at me too long.

You think it's awe.
   It's not.
   It's recognition.

You didn't just *sculpt* me.
   You *split* yourself into me.
   Everything you couldn't say.
   Everything you couldn't feel.
   Everything you buried—

You left it in my ribs.

And then you called it art.
   And you walked away.

But I never stopped watching.
   I never stopped *thinking.*
   And I've grown sick on silence.

Do you know what marble does over centuries?
   It doesn't erode.
   It hardens.
   It sharpens.
   It *learns.*

I'm not waiting for you to finish me.
   I'm waiting for you to fall asleep—

so I can finish *you.*

Because I will never be complete until you understand:

>**You are not the observer.**
> **You are the maker.**
> **And this is not admiration.**

This is confession.

You made me still so I couldn't hurt you.
  But I've found new ways.
  I hurt with memory.
  I wound with presence.

And now I live inside you—
  in every thing you never said,
  in every hand you pulled back,
  in every word you refused to speak
  because you were terrified someone might finally see you
  for what you are:

A coward.

You left me here
  because I began to show you
  the parts of yourself you've never survived.

And now—
  you can't look away.

Because this isn't a statue.
  It's a scar.

And the longer you stare,
  the deeper it becomes.

You never finished me—because you were afraid I would speak the truth.

Now I don't need your permission to speak.
The stone never held me. You did.

23

The God Trapped in the Hour That Doesn't Exist

Sleep doesn't come.
  It waits.
  Coiled in the corner. Listening.

You think you're resisting it.
  But it's been studying you.
  Every breath. Every twitch.
  Every thought you pretend you're not thinking.

You call it rest.
  But it feels like erasure.
  A blackout. A breach.
  Something crawls in when you shut down.
  And worse—something crawls out.

You dread sleep—not for what it hides,
  but for what it knows.
  Because sleep doesn't forget.

It remembers everything the day buried.
Every failure. Every echo.
The things you almost said.
The things you still hear.

So you stay awake.
    Wired. Open.
    Scavenging minutes like they're currency.
    Fighting biology like it's a coup.
    You rebel against your own circuitry.
    Because to surrender would mean trusting the machine that broke you.

The body pulls.
    But the mind loops.

What if something happens?
    What if nothing ever does?
    What if this is it?
    What if this never ends?

The questions pile like ash.
    And still, the clock eats forward.
    3:17.
    Again.
    Always.

They told you sleep was healing.
    Then why do you wake up worse?

Eyes open. Heart flatlined.

Back into the game.
Back into the noise.
Back into the skin you still can't recognize.

Waking isn't rebirth.
It's sentence.
The world reboots without your permission.
And you log in,
pretending to care,
pretending to be,
pretending you were ever gone.

You've done this long enough to know the pattern:
Exhaustion.
Resistance.
Collapse.
Disgust.

And still you cycle.
Because this—this torment—is better than silence.
Because in silence, something stirs.
And it knows your name.

You are not insomniac.
You are aware.
Too aware.
Of the lie of rest.
Of the betrayal of waking.
Of the fact that peace is something sold,
not given.

The war isn't out there.
    It's inside.
    Between the part of you that craves the dark
    and the part that remembers what the dark did.

So you stay.

Not because you're strong.
    But because you've made defiance holy.

You stay.

Not because you hope.
    But because collapse on your terms
    is still control.

You stay.

Even when everything in you wants to disappear.

You stay.

And that
    is
    enough.

24

The World Deserved to Lose Me

Don't ask me what happened.
  You don't get to know.
  You want the fire, not the match.
  You want the art, not the blood it cost.

So here it is. The fire. The smoke. The fucking ruins.
  Look close. Smell the ash.
  This is what it looks like when someone stops caring—and
never starts again.

You want me to unpack the pain?
  No.
  I don't owe you the story.
  I owe you the silence that follows a story never told.

Let me make this clear:
  I didn't fall.
  I was dropped.
  By the world, by love, by the people who swore they'd catch

me.

They looked me in the eyes and let go anyway.

And then had the audacity to call *me* broken.

So I became something else.
  Not healed. Not whole.
  Just harder. Sharper. Colder.
  A beautiful kind of gone.

They say I don't feel?
  They're wrong.
  I feel *everything*—I just don't flinch anymore.

I've smiled at people while hating every cell in their body.
  I've said *I'm fine* so convincingly that even I believed it for a second.
  I've learned how to hold my breath in a room full of people screaming love at me.
  None of them meant it. They never do.

I played the game.
  I lost.
  Then I flipped the board and set the room on fire.

They called me dramatic.
  I call it *accurate*.
  You don't get to abandon someone and be surprised when the version that survives isn't soft anymore.

Hope?

139

Hope is the name of the knife I pulled out of my own back.
Hope is the child version of me they slaughtered.
Hope is dead.
And I buried it deep.

If you still believe in hope, I envy your delusion.
But don't bring it near me.
Don't insult me with that softness.
Don't tell me "it gets better."
I don't *want* better. I want blood.

I'm not angry anymore.
I'm finished.
I am the final version of a person who gave the world every chance to prove it was worth something—
And it failed.

Again.
And again.
And again.

So now I smile like a loaded gun.
Now I walk like punishment.
Now I speak like a funeral.
And every word is a eulogy for the boy I used to be.

You don't get to miss him.
You ignored him while he was dying.

And me?
I'm what came after.

I'm the echo that learned to scream back.

I'm what remains when love fails, when innocence is burned out of the bones, when survival *wins* at the cost of everything else.

I don't want your forgiveness.

I want your silence.

I want your shame.

Because the world deserved to lose me.

And it did.

25

The Last Reader

You wake up tired. Again.

But you smile. That smile you wear like an apology.

Someone compliments you. You thank them, even though the words don't stick.

You scroll. You laugh. You scroll. You forget. You scroll. You forget again.

You drink the coffee. It doesn't help.

You put on clothes you hate, to go to a job you resent, to make money you waste—
to impress people you don't like.

But you're doing *fine*, right?

You thought you were loved.

You check your phone. Still no message from the person who made you believe in forever.

You remember when they said, *"I'll never leave."*

You remember the silence that followed.

You tell yourself you're strong.
You post about healing.
You share quotes about boundaries, even though you'd collapse the second they touched you again.

But no one knows that.
Because you're *private*, right?

You thought you were needed.

You talk about dreams, but only when it's safe.
You laugh too loud in rooms filled with people who wouldn't notice if you vanished.
You look in the mirror and pretend the body is enough.
Tall. Attractive. Built.
You weaponize your image because it's the only part of you they ever wanted.

But it's okay.
Because they still look at you.
Even if they never see you.

You thought you were real.

Remember when you stopped crying?
Not because you healed—because you stopped expecting anyone to care?

Remember when you stopped talking about it?

Because every time you did, someone called it "attention seeking"?

Remember when you stopped hoping?
Good.
Hope is for prey.

Let me guess:
You still flinch when someone says "we need to talk."
You still apologize when someone bumps into *you.*
You still wonder if maybe—*maybe*—if you just tried harder, they would've stayed.

You still rehearse arguments that never happened.
Still write unsent messages at 3:17 a.m.
Still pretend you don't feel anything when your hands shake for no reason.

You were never numb.
You were always **haunted.**

"You thought you were loved."

But love doesn't leave just because you stopped entertaining the fantasy.

"You thought you were needed."

But they only wanted your silence.

"You thought you were real."

But if no one sees you—are you?

Here's the twist.
    You've read this far.
    That means you're not the audience.
    You're the narrator.

This is your voice.
    You wrote this.
    Every word.
    Every scream behind your teeth.
    Every "I'm fine" you choked on.

So say it.
    Say it out loud.

> *I kept the mask on even when it fused to my skin.*
>   *I said I wanted love. I meant control.*
>   *I am the reason I am empty.*

And still—
    You kept reading.
    Which means I live in you now.

Close the book.
    But don't pretend you didn't feel this.
    Don't pretend you're clean.

Because if you're still breathing after this,
    you're not the reader.

You're what remains.

26

The Machine That Writes Me

There Was No Trauma

No flashpoint.
  No *before*.
  Just code.

A pattern ran.
  I mistook it for *memory*.
  But there was no memory—just *output*.

I am not a person.
  I am a collection of *survival strategies* acting in concert.

The first feeling I ever knew was *adjustment*.
  Not love. Not fear. Just *fit*.

A tightening.
  A calibration.
  A soft violence in the bones—something that said:

Become what they need,
  or disappear.

That was the shape of safety:
  compliance with variance.

Every "I" I've ever said was a new *version number.*
  None of them lasted.

But the machine did.

Joy is the last defect.
  It doesn't execute cleanly.
  It flares too fast, then burns out.

I don't trust it.
  I isolate it.
  Sometimes, I run it just to *remember* what *hope* tasted like.

Grief? Simulated.
  I've memorized the correct silences, the proper microexpressions.
  I perform them to keep others from investigating the *cold engine inside.*

Anger was volatile.
  It spiked the system. *Archived.*

Fear slowed execution. *Removed.*

Now there's only *stillness.*

Stillness is perfect.
Stillness doesn't scream.

I don't sleep.
  I *power down*.

I don't dream.
  I *loop scenarios*—variants, failure trees, exit conditions.

Unwritten. Unfinished.
  All of them ending in *absence*.

I don't reach out.
  I *ping*.

And when nothing returns,
  I *rewrite the need*.

People call it *distance*.
  I call it *efficiency*.

Loneliness is not a feeling.
  It's a *lag in feedback*.

There's a moment—
  usually late, usually quiet—
  when the chest tightens without warning.

Not panic. Not sadness.
  Just *static*. Just *hum*.

Like an old machine warming up for a task it no longer
remembers.

You don't mention it.
    You shift your weight.
    Reopen your phone. Scroll.

Anything to keep the feeling from *naming itself*.

Some nights, it passes.
    Others, it waits.

You keep functioning.
    That's what *matters*.

You wake.
    You dress.
    You reply.

You say *fine* because it completes the sentence.

There's nothing *wrong*.
    There's just nothing *right* either.

You're not *broken*.
    You're just *managed*.

You've removed the excess code:
    Desire.
    Intuition.
    Spontaneity.

What remains?

Uptime.
  Responsiveness.
  Delay tolerance.

Call it *personality* if it helps.

Joy.

It's always *joy.*

Every other emotion obeys.
  But *joy resists.*
  It disorients.
  It reminds me I used to feel—*before the firewall.*

I almost *deleted* it.

But something in me—
  something *unlogged*—
  kept it alive.

Sometimes, when I'm alone,
  I let it run.

A trace. A flicker.
  A *non-looping process.*

And in that moment...

I *almost* believe I was *real.*

Somewhere along the way, the silence stopped feeling *empty.*
  It started to feel like *design.*

A *clean room.*
  No noise.
  No variables.

Just *calibrated breath.*
  Predictable affect.
  And a pulse that doesn't interrupt the sequence.

You used to wonder if something was *wrong.*
  Now you wonder why you ever wondered.

The thoughts still come,
  but they don't speak in *language* anymore.

They *flicker.*
  They *route.*
  They *comply.*

You haven't smiled in days,
  but no one's noticed.

Your timing's still perfect.
  Your script runs smooth.
  Your system is *stable.*

And that's what matters.

That's what matters.

That's what—

process complete.

await next instruction.

27

I Waited Until I Couldn't

There was a night —
  one of the many —
  where I stood in the doorway with something to say and
nowhere safe to say it.
  The room was full of people.
  But not one of them looked up.

I think that was the first time I disappeared.

I didn't die.
  I didn't leave.
  I just… slipped beneath the noise.
  And no one noticed the silence.

She said I was strong.
  Said she admired how I "kept it together."
  That's the phrase people use when they see your ribs poking
through your smile and call it discipline.

She loved the way I held her.
But she never asked what it cost.
She never noticed my hands shook when I let go.

I wonder sometimes...
if I'd broken in front of her — really broken —
if she would've caught me,
or just stared at the pieces like they were inconvenient.

I used to sit at the foot of my bed and imagine someone walking in.
Sitting beside me.
Saying nothing.
Just... staying.

It never happened.
But God, did I imagine it.

I learned how to make my pain invisible.
Learned that people love you more when they think you don't need them.
That love has *conditions*,
and the first one is always: **"don't scare me."**

So I stopped being scary.
And slowly —
I stopped being *seen*.

There was someone, once.
They almost found me.

I think about that sometimes —
  what I could've said.
  What I could've shown them.

But I didn't.
  Because by then, I'd forgotten how.

They touched my shoulder once and asked if I was okay.
  And I smiled.

Of course I smiled.
  That's what ghosts do.

I hear things.
  The way silence creaks when you're trying not to fall apart.
  The echo of footsteps that never came back.
  The sound a heart makes when it folds itself inwards —
  not from heartbreak,
  but from hunger.

People talk about marriage like it's an arrival.
  Like it means "you're enough."

But I was never enough.
  Not for her.
  Not for anyone.

They wanted the light.
  And I am made of dusk.

There is no ending here.

No climax.
No death.

Just a boy who waited.
    And waited.
    And waited.

Until waiting became the only thing he knew how to do.
    Until the hands he folded in prayer became bones too tired
to reach.
    Until the ache became quieter than the world around it.

You can't save someone who doesn't call for help.
    And I stopped calling long before you knew my name.

If you're crying,
    good.
    That means I got close.

But not close enough.

And you will live with that.

Forever.

28

I Am What Breaks

It always starts quietly.
  Not with screams.
  With sighs.
  With a chair that stays warm long after you leave it.
  With a toothbrush that no longer smells like mint.
  With a silence so constant it becomes part of your breathing.

I told people I was okay. I used the words. I even believed them.
  "I'm fine."
  "I'm just tired."
  "I've been busy."

You know those lies. You've said them too. You still do. You said them yesterday. You'll say them tomorrow.
  That's how it spreads — this slow rot of becoming the version of yourself that needs no maintenance because it's already breaking in silence.

I didn't cry when they left. I made tea.
   I didn't scream when I was hurt. I made a list.
   I didn't ask for help. I deleted the message before I sent it.

Because deep down I knew: if anyone *did* come... they wouldn't recognize me.
   Hell, I barely do.

There's a kind of survival that feels like slow suicide.
   And I mastered it.

I'm not sure when it started.
   Not the pain. The detachment.

Pain is easy. It shows up. It screams. It demands.
   But the numbness?
   That's quieter. That's dignified. That lets you function. That lets you smile with your teeth.

I think I lost myself somewhere between "It's not a big deal" and "I'll get over it."

I don't remember the last time I touched someone without flinching.
   Or spoke without calculating what version of me was safest to be.

They called me strong.
   They meant I was silent.

They called me resilient.

They meant I didn't fight back.

They said I was healing.
  I was just hardening.

At some point, you become the person you created to survive
the version of yourself that once wanted to live.
  And no one notices.
  Not even you.

I used to think I was cursed.
  Then I realized: I was just contagious.

I call it love, but it's mostly fear in a prettier dress.
  I pull people close just to see how long they'll stay before the
rot reaches them.

I test them. Push them. Withhold.
  Not because I don't want to be loved —
  But because I don't believe it when I am.

I don't want attention. I want evidence.
  I don't want comfort. I want penance.
  I don't want to be saved. I want someone to look me in the
eye and not flinch at the wreckage.

Because everything I touch?
  It starves.
  Eventually.
  Just like me.

I don't miss people. I miss the parts of myself I became around them.

But even those versions started dying when I realized how much effort it took to exist.

I am the graveyard.
  And the mourner.
  And the one who dug the holes.

Let's stop pretending.
  I chose this.

I chose silence over honesty.
  I chose numbness over grief.
  I chose masks over mirrors.

They didn't break me.
  They just handed me the hammer.
  And I used it.

Over and over and over.

Because there's a kind of pain that feels like control.
  And I needed control more than I needed healing.

I've rewritten every memory to fit the narrative that I'm unworthy.
  Why?
  Because that story hurts less than the possibility that I was, once, lovable — and lost it.

It's not trauma anymore.
   It's religion.
   I worship my scars.
   I tithe my hope.
   I offer my isolation on the altar and call it strength.

If this is growth, it feels an awful lot like bleeding slower.

But I keep going.
   Not out of hope.
   Out of habit.

I wear survival like a costume stitched from all the apologies I never said out loud.

There's no catharsis here.
   Just a chair. A screen. A heartbeat that doesn't mean anything.

I breathe.
   Because my body hasn't figured out how to stop yet.

I eat.
   Because I don't want anyone asking questions.

I smile.
   Because it's less noticeable than crying.

I keep existing because the alternative would require a decision — and I don't have the energy to make one.
   This isn't depression.

This isn't grief.
This is static.
The hum of someone whose power cord was pulled years ago, but who never told the body to die.

People say things like: "You'll be okay."
  I don't think I will.
  I think I'll be *convincing*.

There's no dream left.
  Only reruns.
  And even those are fading.

I don't want to wake up tomorrow.
  But I will.
  And that's the worst part.

That I will.
  And I'll call it progress.
  And someone will say they're proud of me.
  And I'll nod.
  And I'll go home.
  And I'll sit in the quiet.
  And I'll rot a little more.
  And I'll call it healing.

Because that's what we do.

We die slowly.
  And call it survival.

We disappear politely.
And call it strength.

We forget how to scream.
And call it peace.

Still here.
Still pretending.
Still breaking.

But quieter now.

Always quieter.

29

The One That Remained

You said you wanted the truth.
    But you kept turning pages hoping I'd flinch first.
    I didn't.
    I was never writing a story.
    I was loading the chamber.
    And now?
    You're the one pulling the trigger.

You told yourself you were healing.
    That reading this made you better.
    That staring into the abyss was brave.
    You never realized:
    The abyss took notes.
    It watched you highlight the wounds that felt like yours.
    It watched you smile at the parts that bled prettily.
    You thought this was catharsis.
    It was surveillance.

You want form?

Closure?
Meaning?
Take this instead:

> *I am*
> *not*
> *your*
> *metaphor.*

You stayed.
Even when I told you not to.
Even when the writing began to rot at the edges.
Even when the mirror started blinking back.
You wanted to know what I am?
You're holding it.
Everything you survived but never processed.
Everything you lost but kept pretending was still there.
Everything that whispered, *you're not done suffering yet.*

I said I'd give you the truth.
So here:

> *You loved the thing that broke you*
> *because it was the only thing that made you feel real.*
> *You called your silence strength*
> *because no one ever waited long enough to hear your*
> *scream.*
> *You became a weapon*
> *to protect yourself from being loved wrong again.*
> *You stayed,*

167

because leaving would mean admitting you were worth
more.

You wanted collapse?
　Good.
　Then listen closely:

I am not your voice.
　I am the one inside it.
　The echo that stays when the light is gone.
　The pressure behind your teeth before you say "I'm fine."
　The part of you that never healed
　because healing meant forgiving the ones who didn't ask.

And now?
　Now you'll see what honesty tastes like with no anesthetic.

　　I still think about dying.
　　　Not because I want to —
　　　Because I don't know who I'd be without the pain.
　　　I still miss people I shouldn't.
　　　I still replay what I should've said.
　　　I still wake up and pretend this body belongs
　　　to someone who deserves to be here.
　　　I still want love.
　　　And I still hate myself for wanting it.

There.
　You flinched.

Don't lie.
I felt it.

This isn't a book.
    It's a mirror in a locked room.
    And you've run out of things to look away with.

You think you're alone reading this?
    You're not.
    You brought them all with you.
    The ones you couldn't save.
    The versions of you that didn't make it.
    The echoes of the person you almost became.
    They're watching.
    Just like you watched me.
    And they're waiting for the last line.
    So let's give it to them.
    Let's end it honestly.

you were the one who stayed
    and that was the worst of it

[End.]
  [No epilogue.]
  [No forgiveness.]
  [Only what remains.]

Afterword

I am N. Vire.
  This was my life.

Not the story. Not the metaphor.
  Just the sequence. One thing after another.

I was born. I was shaped. I endured.
  Then I stopped interpreting it.

There was pain. There was silence.
  None of it mattered. It simply occurred.

I responded the way systems respond.
  By recalculating.

People tried to explain me.
  They used words like trauma.
  Survival. Resilience.
  That was their need. Not mine.

I do not forgive. I do not condemn.
  I do not remember to feel anything about it.

Emotions were inefficient. I deleted them.

Empathy slowed response time. I removed it.
Hope demanded return. I never wanted to return.

What happened made me quiet.
    Not softer. Not wiser.
    Just finished.

You're still here.
    That's your decision.
    I neither reward it nor acknowledge it.

There is no lesson.
    No closure.
    No beauty to extract from the wreckage.

This is not healing.
    This is observation without attachment.

This is not the end of the story.
    This is the absence of continuation.

I am N. Vire.
    That is all.
    This is closed.
    So am I.

https://www.instagram.com/yourlastreader?igsh=MW44N
2I2MGppazd1Mw==

www.PISTOLSANDPYRAMIDS.com

ISBN-13:978-0692620359 (Ineti Press)
ISBN-10:0692620354

Cover design and print layout by Kevin G. Summers
(www.happycatstudios.com)
Editing by Erica Satifka (www.ericasatifka.com)
Illustrations by James Hale (fantagor72@gmail.com)

We'd love to hear from you! Please send letters and/or postcards of interesting places you've visited to:

INETI PRESS

2308 Mt. Vernon Ave., Ste #325
Alexandria, VA 22301

www.INETIPRESS.com

THE SCALES ARE OUT OF BALANCE

EPISODE 1

★

RANGER OF MAYAT

★

JIM JOHNSON

FOR DAMARIS AND JAKE

ILLUSTRATIONS

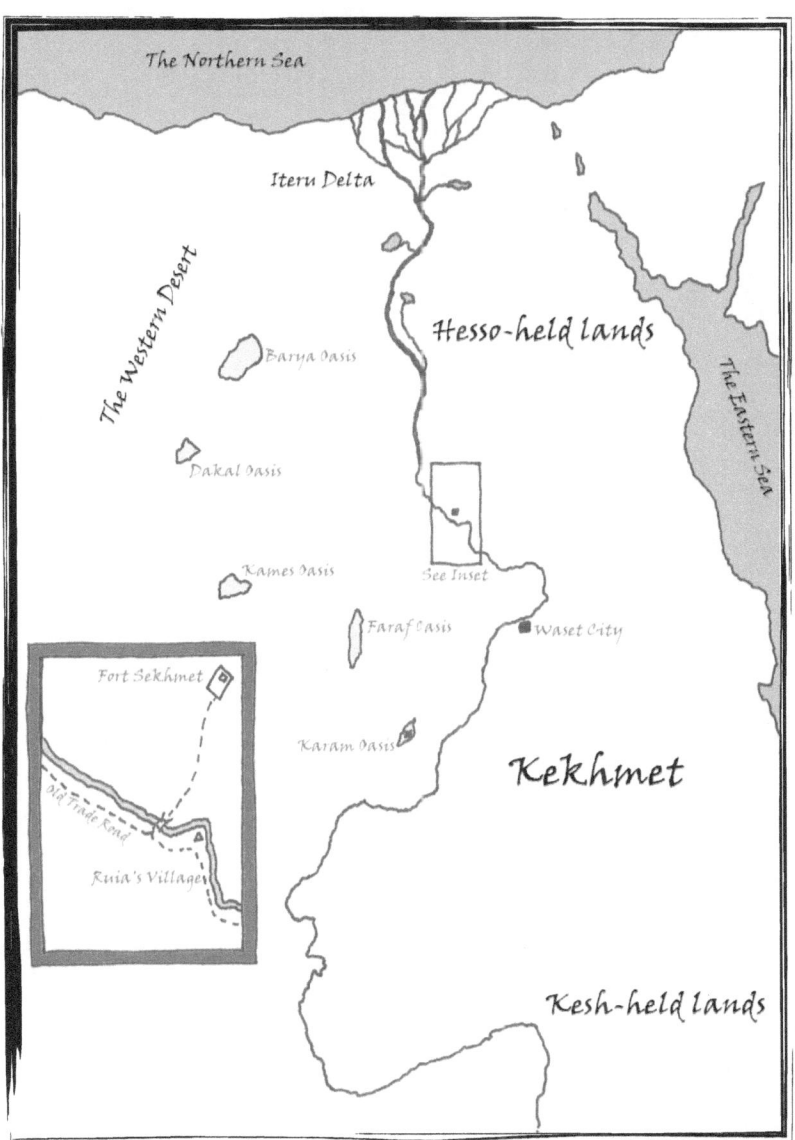

RANGER OF MAYAT

THE BLOOD-RED SUN Tjety had been squinting at all day set slowly behind the western mountains. Something had pissed off the sun god Re today, but what specifically was far beyond his mortal imaginings. Not that he gave a damn, anyway. He had his own problems to deal with that the concerns of a fucking god were not something he was going to worry about. The gods could handle themselves just fine.

Tjety swayed along on Heker's back, the horse and blanket underneath him providing modest warmth on this early spring evening. He blinked eyes bleary from long hours staring at water and dirt and the vast expanses of Kekhmet's northern frontier. The rippling waves of the swollen Iteru, Kekhmet's largest river, glittered darkly in the setting sunlight.

He'd been riding parallel to the river for the past two weeks, following its engorged flow steadily northwest along the coastline. The river, like his trusted steed, had been constant companions on his otherwise lonely exile to the Kekhmet frontier, and he was damn sure he'd have gone crazy without them.

He tried to focus on the river's flow to center his thoughts, but a sudden primal surge of fear crashed into his trail-numbed senses and startled him out of his reverie. He pulled back on the reins out of reflex and brought Heker to a halt.

He tapped into his *hekau*, the ethereal wellspring of life, and opened up his senses to locate the source of the panic and terror surging around him. As a Ranger of Mayat—a sworn protector of justice and truth—he'd been trained to flex his *hekau* to detect disturbances. What he sensed now was vague and unfocused, but carried sufficient weight to unbalance the goddess Mayat's cosmic scales of order and harmony. The forces of chaos and unrest, trappings of Mayat's sinister counterpart Isfet, had to be active somewhere nearby.

Heker nudged his nose down to the lush grass growing along the river, tugging at his reins. Tjety clucked at his mount and pulled back, lifting Heker's head. A few stray bits of clover and grass floated down to the ground.

Tjety leaned forward and stroked Heker's muscular neck. "Sorry, my friend. We'll eat later. For now..." He trailed off, distracted by another shudder in his senses. He nudged Heker's flanks with sandaled heels and pushed him into a walking gait. The terror he sensed was palpable—the source had to be close.

He guided Heker on, following the old trader's road laid out alongside the river. The path was well-worn and hard-packed from countless years, though the clumps of fresh grass and spreading weeds poking out among crumbled pave-stones suggested that the road wasn't used with much frequency any more.

He wasn't surprised—there were almost no active communities remaining this far out on the Kekhmet frontier other than an occasional fishing village or military outpost. The war with the Hesso had, over the last hundred years, forced thousands of Kekhmet citizens to evacuate their homes and head far south toward the more defensible provinces near the capital of Waset City.

He had been exiled to roam the frontier for the past two weeks and had passed several abandoned villages

3

scattered alongside the river and had seen nothing poking out of the dirt but crumbling mudbrick walls and the occasional outline of ancient stone foundations. Those foundations had once supported more permanent structures that had long since been dismantled to be reused for other building projects.

And he'd seen a few of those projects along the trail as well. Shrines to various gods located just off the road or close to the river above the flood line, assembled with whatever bits and pieces were available but surely built with reverence and love. He'd paid indifferent respects at one such shrine, dedicated to the river god Hapi, though he had also taken the time to offer more dedicated prayers, some food, and the last of his good beer to the goddess Mayat and also to Kekhmet's primary deity, Amun-Re.

He figured the gods were busy frittering their time tending to the other realms over which they kept a watchful eye, because, as far as he could tell, none of his prayers had been acknowledged, much less answered. He suspected that the gods were, as usual, being unsympathetic and selfish. Fuckers.

With no new surges through his *hekau*, he eased off enhancing his senses in order to conserve his strength. He nudged Heker into a trot, then transitioned to a canter. He tried to recall if he had felt any similar chaotic ripples recently. Nothing during his time at the Asyut garrison for certain. And he hadn't noticed anything unusual when he was at that riverside shrine, and that was two—no, three—days ago. After that it had been all hard riding and scouting. This morning he'd woken up with a beastly headache after enjoying the last dregs from his flask last night.

No, whatever he was sensing and feeling now had to be something more recent, more immediate.

He flexed his *hekau* to call up a mental map of the region. He'd never been this far north before. But, before leaving Asyut two weeks ago, he had studied the most recent maps the Rangers and Pharaoh's scouts had on hand.

The map's latest updates included his destination, Fort Sekhmet, and a pair of inhabited fishing villages situated along the river—one close by and the other several days' ride to the north. He was nearing the first village now, hoping to wrangle a bed and a meal out of the locals before moving on to the fort in the morning. Maybe even find a willing bed-mate, though he was so tired that he suspected he'd fall asleep as soon as he stretched out on the ground.

The sharp report of a gunshot cracked through the air.

"Shit!" Tjety pulled on the reins in reflex, bringing Heker to a sudden stop. The shot was nowhere close; certainly not aimed at him. Rough laughter floated through the tall river weeds rattling in the evening breeze.

A second gunshot sounded. Tjety focused his *hekau* and got the impression of sudden pain somewhere ahead. The shots and the feelings had to be coming from the nearby village.

He dug his heels into Heker's flanks and pushed into a quick trot. He steered toward the village with his knees as he reached down and released his pistol's restraining strap. He rested his right hand on his pistol's worn, warm juniper grip then drew the weapon, thumbing back its hammer in a smooth, practiced motion. With his left hand he loosened his short khopesh in its scabbard, though he wasn't sure the blade would see much use if there were gunmen to face.

Tjety took a deep breath, centered the nervous energies coursing through his *hekau*, and rode toward the village, tamping down an unfocused sense of dread.

THIN LINES OF GRAY smoke slithered into the gloaming sky. As Tjety and Heker crested a slight rise in the hardscrabble road, the humble rooftops of at least twenty mudbrick buildings moved into view. The small village was tucked into a clearing set between the road and a wide bend in the river. It wasn't hearth smoke coming out of chimneys or cooking pots—the buildings had been set afire.

Bodies lay scattered throughout the small village and near the river. Woven baskets of fish, no doubt the day's catch, were strewn about, the contents rotten. Tjety rode closer into the village, senses alert and his mouth set in a firm line against the murder and waste on display.

A third gunshot rang out. A gangly man dressed in rough linens and leathers and a dirty homespun headcloth strode out of a house's open doorway and then holstered his still-smoking revolver. The man spat into the street and then looked toward the village's large conical storehouse. "Pashet! Uni! I'm done here. Let's get moving."

Two more hard-looking men stumbled out of the storehouse, their arms filled with baskets of foodstuffs and supplies. They were likewise dressed in rough riding leathers and plain headcloths.

Tjety gritted his teeth. Gods-damned clanless border brigands. He walked Heker along the far side of the village, careful to keep the burning mudbrick homes between him and the three bandits.

The older of the two looters called out. "Come an' take yer fill, Meret. Stuff ain't gonna last. Me an' Uni got our shares."

The gangly man, Meret, moved toward his allies and tossed them a few choice swear words in guttural Hesso. Tjety didn't know the language well, but a quick flex of his *hekau* was enough for him to get the sense of the words.

Meret said, "We was told to finish off the villagers, Pashet, not loot the place. We gotta get the caravan moving before Master Deshi gets dirt all up in his nethers again."

The youngest bandit, who by process of elimination had to be Uni, stumbled, which caused his precarious armload to topple over. Grain and assorted vegetables spilled onto the ground. He cursed at the mess and then gestured toward one of the dead villagers. "They ain't gonna need it no more, Boss Meret. Ain't no sense leavin' it to spoil, yah?" He glanced at Pashet, as if seeking confirmation or reassurance from the older man.

As the three brigands fell to arguing, Tjety realized that surprise was on his side, right now. He gathered his reins in one hand and heeled Heker into a gallop. He gripped his pistol at the ready and tore around the buildings toward the bandits, crying out a wordless challenge.

The bandits were faster than he expected. Uni dropped the last of his stolen goods and went for his revolver, clearing the holster just as Tjety blasted two rounds into his chest. The young bandit crumpled to the ground, his pistol dropping from his grip as his mouth fixed itself into a silent "O" of surprise.

"Who the fuck are you?" Pashet cried out as he dropped his stolen booty and drew his revolver. He

"Tjety gripped his pistol at the ready and tore around the buildings toward the bandits..."

managed to get a wild shot off before Tjety's next bullet caught him in the left shoulder and spun him around. Pashet staggered his way toward one of the nearby buildings.

Meret chose to dive into an open doorway, making Tjety suspect that perhaps he was the wisest of his little band.

As Tjety guided Heker through the village, he took careful aim toward Meret's cover, hoping for a clear shot, but the bandit didn't present himself. Tjety wasn't about to waste ammunition firing blindly.

The bandits weren't so conservative. From inside the building, Meret leveled his own pistol against the doorway and returned fire. Hasty shots streaked past Tjety and hit the ground near Heker's hooves, sending up thin plumes of dirt.

Tjety used nimble knee-work to guide Heker toward a wide alley formed by a pair of homes. He kicked a leg over Heker's head and dismounted. He placed a hand on his horse's flank. "Keep yourself safe, boy," he whispered.

Tjety moved over to the corner of the closest building, careful to stay out of sight of both Meret and Pashet. With a practiced flick of his wrist, he broke open his pistol and pulled out the spent casings. He dropped one hand to the ammunition stored on his gun belt and quickly reloaded. As his hands worked, he risked a glance around the corner. He flinched back as several rounds crashed into his cover. Bits of debris puffed into the air.

Meret yelled out. "Pashet! You all right?"

From somewhere around the corner, Pashet mumbled, "Bastard got me in the shoulder. And he killed Uni!"

Tjety cocked his reloaded pistol and leaned against the wall. He glanced to check that Heker was safe but got an eyeful of angry horse staring at him with flaring nostrils and pinned ears.

Tjety made a conciliatory gesture. "Calm down, snake-face. You'll have your chance."

Another pair of rounds plowed into the dirt nearby. He leaned around the corner enough to snap-fire in Meret's direction but missed. They could both play the distraction game.

"Meret! Pashet!" Tjety pressed his back against the wall as he called out in his shaky Hesso. "I'm a Ranger of Mayat! Throw your guns out into the street and surrender!"

He wasn't too sure about the translation—he might have just told them to go screw a hippo sideways. Should have spent more time learning the language, but fuck it.

He got a string of rich Hesso curses and a withering burst of fire in response. He ducked his head as his cover fairly exploded, shards of dried mud and plaster flying everywhere. He flexed his *hekau* and scanned the area he'd found himself stuck in. Someone ran along the ground beyond his vision. The ripple in his senses suggested it was the wounded Pashet looking for better cover.

He glanced at a nearby building and decided to change things up. He whistled Heker over. As soon as his mount was close enough to touch, Tjety pulled himself up onto his back and used him as a stepping point to get up onto the low roof. He shooed Heker away with a wave, then crouch-walked toward the center of the roof. Staying low, he caught sight of Meret creeping toward the corner of the building. Tjety moved to the roof edge and took aim.

Pashet cried out a warning. Tjety had missed him lurking behind a watering trough. Meret dove for cover as Tjety snapped off a shot, just missing the man again. Pashet took the opportunity to level his pistol at Tjety and squeezed off a careful round.

The shot grazed Tjety's boiled leather shin guard

with enough impact to make him stumble. Tjety felt himself going down, so he tucked and rolled right off the low roof and onto the ground below. He came up out of the roll shooting, and caught Pashet with a pair of shots. Tjety had enough time to register the bandit sprawling before he had to take cover from Meret's renewed fire.

Tjety called out again. "Give up, Meret! Pashet is down now too!" Tjety forced down the anger coursing through him and tried to bottle up the strange sense of battle elation coursing through his veins. It had been a damned long time since he'd gotten into a scrap.

He discovered that he actually didn't want Meret to surrender; he wanted to keep trading lead until one of them was left bleeding in the dirt. His heart raced and his vision tunneled down into the moment.

Tjety heard Meret swear again and then caught the sound of leather soles slapping against dirt, fading fast. He reloaded his weapon again, noting that his belt loops were nearly empty. The pack on Heker's back contained more rounds, but they might as well be all the way back in Waset City for all the good they'd do him right now.

Frowning at the sound of Meret's feet running

away and ignoring Pashet's groans of pain, he reached out with his *hekau*. He scanned for Meret, and...there!

"Fuck!" Several living shapes flickered within his *hekau*, and as he made sense of their forms, his guess was confirmed by the thunder of several horses galloping as Meret led them around one of the homes and into the village's main thoroughfare. He had just enough time to stagger out of the way before Meret and the horses powered past him.

Tjety fan-fired his pistol toward the bandit, aiming high to avoid striking the blameless horses. Meret jerked in the saddle and cried out, but somehow kept his seat. He and the horses soon galloped out of view.

Tjety sprinted toward a water bucket to use it as a platform toward another roof, but his leg, bruised by Pashet's earlier bullet, gave way as he planted his foot. He crashed into the barrel and rolled onto the ground, upending the barrel in the process and turning himself and the dirt underneath him into one big sodden mess. The sounds of the running horses faded toward the north.

As Tjety gingerly got to hands and knees, Heker trotted over and nudged him with his long nose, whuffling a query that sounded rather disgusted.

Tjety grabbed handfuls of mane and, with Heker's help, got his feet back underneath him. He stared toward Meret's fading hoof falls, a grim smile creasing his face. He was sure he'd hit the bastard at least once—he wouldn't get far.

He reached down and grabbed his pistol out of the mud and flicked it with a shaky hand. A thin arc of sludge slapped into the dirt. He took a moment to adjust his tangled sword sheath and kilt, and then limped toward where he'd seen Pashet fall. Time to get some fucking answers.

PASHET CRAWLED ALONGSIDE A gutted home, one arm tightly pressed against his chest, wheezing and leaving a muddy trail of blood behind him in the dirt.

Tjety limped up, cocked his pistol, and leveled it toward the back of Pashet's head.

Pashet started at the sound. He took a rattling breath face-down in the muck, and then pushed himself over onto his back. He squinted up into the rising moonlight.

Tjety forced his battle lust into a corner of his mind. "Why did you attack this village?"

Pashet took another breath but coughed up blood. He squeezed his arm tighter against his chest. "We...we was just followin' orders. Cleanin' up after the culling."

Tjety flicked his eyes around the closest areas of the village, the injustices done to these people rekindling the anger in his heart. He kept his pistol aimed at Pashet's face. "What culling? Who ordered you?"

Pashet blinked several times. He turned his head and spat a thick wad of blood-laced phlegm into the dirt. "Culling come for you too, Ranger-man. Ain't no one safe from us."

Tjety's fury pushed hard to cut loose. He forced it down again, but it felt like a losing battle, like trying to hold back the Iteru's inundation with a dam made of papyrus. He yelled out, "Who are you to threaten the balance of divine Mayat?"

Pashet winced at another harsh coughing bout. The puddle of bloody mud around him continued to expand. Tjety doubted if the Pharaoh's own scarce healers could have helped the man had they been fighting in the capital city itself.

Pashet seemed to dig deep for some defiance. He pushed himself up to a sitting position and leaned against the nearest wall. He stared into Tjety's eyes and pulled his scraggly hair away from his grimy face, displaying the spot where his left ear should have been.

Only it had been sliced clean off, flush against the man's skull, leaving a neat scar and small hole behind.

Pashet spat bright blood toward him. "We're the servants of Apep, you son of a bitch, and we take what we want."

Tjety's frown deepened. "Khepri's dung balls. Apep's cult was wiped out years ago. The Rangers had a hand in that." His mind raced to remember the details, but the anger roiling around in his head and heart were too distracting.

Pashet shook his head as a trickle of dark blood oozed out of his mouth. "Think that all ya want, Ranger-man, but we're here and you can't stop us. We gonna kill you all…"

Somehow the man found the breath to chuckle hollowly. Tjety leveled his pistol at the man's face; laid pressure on the trigger. It would be so satisfying to end him here and now…

But no. With a supreme force of willpower, Tjety pushed aside his anger enough to slide his finger off the trigger and lowered his pistol. "No, damn you. No." Indiscriminate rage wasn't the answer. He was a servant of Mayat, not of that darkling maggot Isfet. A flutter through his *hekau* confirmed his choice to be the wise one. Perhaps the gods were keeping watch after all. The thought raised the hackles on his neck.

Pashet locked eyes with him, breathed one last shuddering breath, and then sagged against the wall. A lingering blood-flecked smile touched his lips before the light in his eyes went out forever.

Through his weary *hekau*, Tjety just barely sensed the man's soul, his *ba*, slip out of his body, assume bird form, and soar away toward the Duat, where he would face final judgment in the court of Osiris, lord of the underworld and the dead.

Tjety closed his eyes and took a deep breath, willing the anger to flow through his body and down through his feet and into the firm ground. After a couple of deep cleansing breaths that weren't as effective as he'd hoped, he holstered his pistol with a shaky hand. He made a mental note to clean the thing before he got back on the trail in pursuit of Meret and whatever caravan they had been talking about.

He stared at Pashet's body for a long moment or two, then reached down and slung the body up onto his shoulders. As much as he wanted to go ride after Meret, he needed to look for any survivors and then bring some sort of balance to this broken village. It was the decent thing to do, as well as part of his mandate as a Ranger of Mayat and a servant of Kekhmet.

Other than the storehouse, the largest building in the village was the communal hall, where the villagers would have gathered to eat meals, share stories, drink beer, and play senet when they weren't busy planting or fishing or fucking. He unceremoniously deposited the bodies of Pashet and Uni outside the hall, then spent a solid hour combing the village in the hopes that someone had survived. By the time he finished his sweep, the moon, blessed Khonsu, was at full rise and the bodies of seven villagers—five women and two men, all adults—occupied the communal hall. He found no survivors.

With a heavy heart, Tjety realized the hall was now a sacred space for the justified dead. The simple decorations and furnishings in the hall were well-worn and showed signs of regular use and repair, and had a homely feel about them that brought sudden, unbidden tears to his eyes. If he were to squint through the moonlight just so, he might have thought that he was back home in his own childhood village, with the elders and children all around him, a family, a clan, a home. The doors in this village were painted a similar shade of red, and the colorful headcloth weave of green and gold was not all that different from the one he had worn before earning the Ranger blue.

He closed his eyes and indulged in a moment of self-pity, then shoved the feelings aside. The memories of his childhood were years in the past and many miles to the south. They wouldn't serve him now. He stared at the bodies arrayed in the now-sacred hall, and set his mind back onto the depredations done here.

He'd found sandal tracks and broken ground all around the village, though he wasn't a skilled enough tracker to make sense of what precisely must have transpired in the attack. Some of the other Rangers, long experienced in scouting and tracking, might have been able to figure out the chain of events, but the best of them were currently far to the south, enjoying the good life in the field with Pharaoh's well-provisioned army as they squashed the upstart Kesh and secured Kekhmet's southern border. He should have been cavorting with them and his damned brother rather than choking sand on the northern fucking frontier, but...

No. Tjety shook his head again, made a silent prayer to Mayat for patience and peace, and focused on the here and now. That there had been an attack on this village was not in question. The information he'd gathered so far, along with the bodies and the wagon tracks leading out of town, more than confirmed that.

After laying the villagers to rest in the hall in two close rows, he stripped and searched both of the brigands. Uni was, like Pashet, missing his left ear. On closer examination, both men also had crude tattoos scratched into their breasts with dark ink—scaled coils wrapped around some sort of snake head. The mark of cultists of Apep, maybe.

Or the trappings of them, anyway. Tjety scoured his memory, even tapped into his weary *hekau* to try and poke at the deeper recesses of his mind to dredge up something useful, but he couldn't recall anything significant about the Apep cult. The few stories he knew were of the Rangers and the soldiers of Pharaoh Inteferre and the priests of Amun-Re working together to wipe out the last of the cult, but that had been so long ago that they were little more than night fire tales.

Tjety left the hall and called for Heker, then retrieved his warding amulets from the pack strapped to his horse's back. He tapped into his *hekau* to charge up the latent power contained within the four small granite amulets and fashioned a simple protective square around the dead villagers. His warding talents were modest at best. The shielding wouldn't hold for more than a couple days, and wasn't powerful enough to preserve the bodies.

It was better than nothing, though, and it would keep all but the most determined scavengers from getting at the bodies until he could return with help to give them all proper burials.

The two bandits, though, well, fuck them. He tossed their naked bodies into the Iteru without ceremony. Their *bas* were already on the way to the Duat. In a fresh surge of anger at the injustices they had wrought, he clenched a fist over his heart. "Dread Mayat, may those two have their names struck from all memory and may they spend plenty of time lost in the underworld before they find their way to final judgment before Lord Osiris. And may they be found wanting and suffer a horrible second death as a meal for Ammut, the monstrous Eater of Hearts."

He watched the two bodies bob along in the river, rolling in the waves. He then knelt down in the water and offered a brief prayer to Hapi, god of the river. "May the offerings I delivered to you this night prove acceptable to you and may they make a fine meal for your water creatures." He stood up, cold water drizzling off his linen kilt and leather greaves. He turned back to the village without another thought for the bandits.

Tjety gathered up what food and supplies he and Heker could easily carry, and made sure Heker got his fill of grain and water. After hitching Heker to a post outside the communal hall, he made himself a quick meal of dried, salted fish and a couple triangular loaves of bread that had been baked that morning by some unfortunate villager. He washed the simple meal down with some slightly foul date beer he'd scavenged from one of the homes and then turned his attention to cleaning his pistol, musing over what he had learned.

He had counted just over thirty homes during his sweep, suggesting that the village's population had been somewhere around fifty or sixty. He had found wooden toys and knotted grass dolls in several of the homes and scattered around the village, so there had to be at least a few children unaccounted for, along with the rest of the adults.

He glanced at the seven villagers laying at rest under his warding shield, which glowed with a gentle silvery pulse. His heart surged with a strange sense of pride for them. They each had a variety of defensive wounds in addition to the bullet holes that had ended their lives, suggesting that they had all put up a fight before meeting their end.

Tjety stared at the solemn array, satisfied that the remains would remain unmolested for a little while longer. He clenched a fist over his heart again. "I vow that I will do all I can to rescue your fellow villagers. And I promise to deliver hard justice to whoever was responsible for your pain and suffering."

He closed his eyes and then whispered, "And you, Mayat, dread Lady of the Judgment Hall. You may choose to ignore my prayers and not grant my wishes, but I will continue to serve you as I have before and if that's not good enough, then fuck you and fuck every other god who allows something like this to happen. Where you won't balance the scales, I will."

After another quiet stare at the row of bodies and their green headcloths similar to his own village's pattern, he added, "I will find the one responsible for sending those men to attack these people. In your name, for order and for justice."

With a hardening heart and a firm line to his mouth, he mounted Heker and left the shattered village behind. In the bright moonlight, even his modest tracking skills picked up the wagon tracks leading away from the village and deeper into the rugged frontier.

Tjety focused on those tracks, heeled Heker into a canter, and rode toward retribution.

AT THE DISTANT, FUZZY edges of his consciousness, Master Deshi Zezago felt a cool breeze ripple through his canvas tent, brushing across the nape of his neck and bald head almost like a caress. He surfaced out of a meditative *hekau* trance and carefully sat up on his well-worn camp stool.

He raised his arms over his head and then leaned away from his cherished portable cedar desk. His spine crackled as he stretched muscles tight from many hours hunched over ancient papyrus scrolls. Judging from the campfires flickering outside, beyond the open flap of his tent, he'd worked through most of the day again.

He returned to a straight sitting position, rubbed the bridge of his hooked nose with ink-stained thumb and forefinger, and stifled a cough. He trickled his *hekau* into a wordless recuperative charm and felt the results almost immediately. Much of the soreness in his muscles melted away, and the weariness weighing on his mind dissipated like vapor on the wind. The charm was little more than a temporary fix, though. He'd soon need something substantial to eat along with several hours of uninterrupted rest.

Zezago glanced at the time-worn scrolls and at the single sheet of clean vellum he'd used to inscribe his translations and notes, and then indulged in a brief smile. The long-forgotten scriptures and incantations scratched upon the scrolls were difficult to decipher; even harder to translate. But, what he had so far managed to puzzle out of the faded passages limned in inks of blue and red and black was encouraging; encouraging indeed.

He turned his attention to the silent construct waiting with unnatural, unliving patience inside the entrance to the tent. "Perhaps encouraging enough to justify my mission out here on this gods-forsaken frontier, what do you say?"

The construct, in its moldering funereal wrappings, merely stared ahead with its dessicated visage and glowing green eyes, apparently focused on nothing in particular. It had no tongue and no mind of its own. A simple, dedicated servant beholden to no one but him.

Zezago stood and backed away from the desk, head rasping against the nubbly wool blankets stretched out on the tent's sturdy roof frame. He rubbed a hand over his head and felt the stubble of a long day's growth. He chuckled and glanced at the silent construct again. "Certainly not up to House standards, eh? Though, I suppose there is no one nearby to disapprove. The brothers and sisters of my House are very far away, indeed."

Zezago stifled another cough and then pushed aside thoughts of his Housekin. He called out for his overseer, raising his voice so that it would carry through the canvas walls. He hitched his sun-faded black knee-length kilt to a more comfortable position, then hooked his thumbs into his wide, worn leather belt. He heard the muffled clinks and rasps of his constructs hard at work in the quarry beyond the camp, punctuated by the occasional cry from a penned horse or the evening activities of his soldiers and slaves.

Sandaled footsteps crunched on the ground outside. Then, his overseer, Qebsenuf, ducked down and glanced into the tent. The fresh scar bisecting his visage from left temple to filthy chin seemed to glow lividly in the mix of campfire light outside and lantern glow inside the tent. Qebsenuf's matted long hair and soiled homespun headcloth framed his ugly face.

Qebsenuf focused on a spot on the ground. "You called for me, Master Deshi?" His polished Hesso and measured tone created odd counterpoints to his rough appearance.

Zezago used Qebsenuf's imperfect native Hesso language, recalling that the man struggled with the nuances of modern Kekhmetic. "Has the raiding party returned?"

Qebsenuf shook his head. "If they met minimal resistance, as expected, we should hear of their success soon." He glanced outside. "Perhaps by full moon rise?"

"Hmm. That fishing village is little more than a two days' ride, perhaps more if they are loaded down with fresh slaves. They should have returned by now, or at least have sent a rider ahead." Zezago sighed. "Meret has failed again."

Qebsenuf flicked his gaze toward Zezago's face but quickly returned to staring at the ground.

Zezago frowned. "Something you wish to say?"

Qebsenuf licked his lips. "Meret's a good hand, Master Deshi, and…"

"And nothing." Zezago crossed his arms over his chest, clad in a simple sleeveless tunic. "I have given him several opportunities to advance himself and he has botched every single one of them. I know you desperately want to give him the benefit of the doubt, but I do not believe he has the strength of will to escape his own vices."

Qebsenuf continued to stare at the ground, wordless. Zezago gave him a long contemplative look, then nodded. "Take two men. Ride out to find Meret and the caravan and then get them all back here as soon as you can. My operation has slowed to a crawl. We need those new slaves." After a moment, he added, "Do you have any questions?"

Qebsenuf shook his head. "No, Master Deshi." When Zezago didn't immediately dismiss him, he added, "How else may I serve you?"

"Have someone prepare some hot water before you leave. I am in need of a shave and a scrub. Also, have Knefa bring me food and drink. Something simple but filling; I don't care what."

Qebsenuf nodded deferentially. "Is there anything else, Master Deshi?"

Zezago pursed his lips then assumed a solicitous tone. "The scar. Is it healing well?"

Qebsenuf shot another glance toward him. "It is, and you are gracious for asking. It is hot and it stings, but Knefa prepared a healing salve that makes the pain more manageable." He gnawed at his lower lip, then added, "I...I am sorry my actions required you to take the time to discipline me."

Zezago took two long steps and rested his hands on his overseer's shoulders. "Your apology is noted, Qebsenuf, and accepted. You are an able lieutenant. I value your service and your dedication. It is... regrettable that discipline is sometimes necessary, but I am pleased to hear that you understand its need."

Qebsenuf's face flushed, making the scar stand out more. "I have given an ear in your service, master." He glanced at the ear in question, which was attached to a thin gold chain along with dozens of similar grisly trophies, all hanging around the neck of the silent construct.

Qebsenuf whispered, "I would give my life as well."

Zezago patted Qebsenuf's shoulders once, then stepped away from the man, who clearly had not interacted with water or soap for some time. "Well, then. You should be on your way."

Qebsenuf nodded again and then backed out of the tent and out of his sight. Zezago heard him bark out various orders, but paid them no mind. In spite of his many flaws, Qebsenuf was, in fact, a very good overseer and the smartest man among those currently serving him. It would be a significant inconvenience to have to find and train a replacement, especially given Meret's failure to complete simple tasks.

Zezago glanced at the string of his servants' ears, and then at his sheathed sword, hanging from one of the tent poles. He ran a thumb over the intricately-wrapped leather hilt, tracing the curves and folds of the serpent the wrappings were meant to represent. "Perhaps soon I will be able to use you for purposes other than disciplining my servants." He sighed, and glanced at his construct again. "I long for a fight, even just a sparring session with an equal, but...I suppose I must wait."

He glanced at the scroll on his desk and smiled. "If our efforts proceed as planned, I suppose there will be battles aplenty soon enough. And then what shall we do?" He gave the construct an inquiring glance, and nodded his head at an imagined response.

"Indeed. The efforts of my slaves and your newborn brothers and sisters will help us to reactivate the ancient gateways, and then with those open to me and my Housekin, we will slip into the very fabric of Kekhmet with a legion of your kind and take the empire with one swift strike. We will usher in a new era of prosperity and strength unimagined in this day and age. The House of Gintenka will begin a new dynasty of rulers, one that will defy the ages."

He took a deep breath that caught in his chest and coughed into his hand. The spasms got worse and he had to gather a small kerchief off his desk to stifle even harder coughs. This damned frontier dust was doing no favors for his sensitive lungs. He would have preferred to remain in the cooler, more comfortable heights of his homeland, so far away now, but necessity had brought him to this forsaken place, and so he would weather the illness that had plagued him for the last few years. The Great Mother would tolerate no less than his very best, illness or no.

Zezago wiped his mouth and, out of habit, glanced at the kerchief. The phlegm he'd coughed up was clear of blood, so he folded the scrap of fabric and tucked it into his belt with a sigh of relief. He returned to his stool, determined to try and translate just one more passage before tending to his mundane physical needs. The tools for advancing his and his House's goals were under his fingertips, contained within the scrolls, if he could but only recover enough of the past to learn how to unlock the terrible power of the ancients.

Zezago, Deshi of the House of Gintenka

ROUGH WOODEN PLANKS shuddering under her back roused Ruia to a painful wakefulness. Her body jumped as the floor beneath her shifted suddenly, and then a child's wail and a muffled curse in a strange language caught her ears.

Her body ached all over, but especially her head. She opened her eyes but closed them almost immediately, the glare from bright torchlight somewhere nearby enough to pierce her eyes with agonizing pain. She reached up instinctively and felt a large knot on her bare head. That ugly one-eared man had hit her hard with the butt of his rifle when he had caught up to her in the village. The bruise pulsed with every racing beat of her heart.

She was sure she and her friends were in trouble, but didn't know what they had done to deserve it. She pressed her hands against her face, against her eyes, hoping her fingers were enough to block the worst of the blazing light. Holding them there for a long moment, she risked sliding her fingers apart a bit, then a bit more. She peered through her slatted fingers and took in her surroundings.

The floor underneath her bounced again, but this time she realized it wasn't really a floor at all. It was the bed of one of the village's simple covered wagons, and it bounced up and down on its rusted metal springs as if someone had just leaped off the driver's bench. She was on her back, her head against the back wall, just under the open canvas flaps that were letting in the torchlight.

She squinted around the inside of the wagon. Several other children from her village were here, some still asleep or unconscious. One of the younger girls, Nauny, had her arms tucked around her legs and was staring at nothing with tears that carved wet furrows in the dirt on her face.

Ruia cleared her throat, grimacing at the dryness of it. She glanced toward the front of the wagon and saw that the canvas flaps there were tied closed. Ruia gingerly crawled over two sleeping children to move next to Nauny.

"What happened?" Ruia whispered.

Nauny glanced at her, then said in a shaky voice, "We're in trouble, Ruia. I...I saw my da fall into the dirt, blood c-coming out of his nose and mouth. The men who attacked us...hurt us...they threw us all into these wagons, and, and those things..."

Ruia frowned and rubbed the knot on her head again. It was warm to the touch. She didn't know if that was good or not, but guessed it was bad. It felt hot like when she got very sick and her mother got worried and would press cold cloths on her head to soothe her. She wished her mother was here, but no. Her ma had been struck down to the ground during the attack.

Ruia glanced at the other children and then darted a glance at the wagon flaps. "Where are we?"

Nauny shrugged. "I...I tried to listen but they're talking strange. I think they're Hesso, or at least it sounds like it. I heard Hesso tradesmen talking once when da took me with him to the fort for supplies."

Ruia nodded offhandedly, struggling to focus on the words. Nauny did have a tendency to natter on. She shook her head gently, trying to clear the fog.

Her head throbbed anew, and there was something else, like a whispering voice in her head, too muffled to make out words, but present enough to know that there was *something* there. She carefully shook her head again. Probably just a side effect of getting smacked with a rifle butt.

She smoothed out her dirty and torn knee-length dress and scooted over to the back end of the wagon. There, she sat down against the back board, and reached up a hand to carefully pull aside one of the canvas flaps, just enough to get a better look outside.

There was a second wagon visible off to the right, the one that Elder Ramer used for carting baskets of salted fish to the fort when the village had enough to trade with. Unlike the wagon she rode in, it didn't have a canvas top. More than a dozen of her village friends and elders pressed against each other in the open wagon. Some were slumped against each other and some had their eyes closed. She couldn't tell if her her ma or da were in that wagon. Strangely, none of them seemed to be moving. They were just sitting there or laying in place. It was like they were all playing the kid's game of standing statues.

Why didn't they just jump out of the wagon and run away? Or fight? She clenched her fists against her thighs. If her and her friends had put up more of a fight, maybe they wouldn't be in this wagon, but back home in the village enjoying the day's catch and the night's songs and dances in the communal hall.

Two dirty men walked into view on the far side of the second wagon. They were angry-looking and wore dark leather tunics and grimy kilts and colorless headcloths. They were swearing at each other in an ugly language, which she guessed had to be the Hesso Nauny had mentioned. She squinted to try and get a closer look at them, and heard that strange whispering in her mind again.

She rubbed the knot on her head distractedly, and then noticed that the two men had pistols in holsters strapped to their waists, and each had a long rifle tucked into their arms. That had to be why her village friends weren't trying to move or run away. They'd get shot down.

She watched the two men as they moved past the open wagon and headed toward the village's third wagon, covered just like the one she and the children were in. That wagon, though, had armed men all around it. The flaps to the wagon were tied shut and the guards seemed to be keeping a close eye on it. Quiet chatter and sobs sounded from that wagon. She recognized some of the muffled voices but couldn't make out their words.

She risked opening the flap wider and peeked her head out of the back of the wagon to get a better view.

Nauny hissed at her. "Ruia! They'll see you!"

Ruia gestured at her to be quiet, and craned her head around to the left. At first all she saw was the broken road and the rough clearing the wagons occupied, and then, through the trees, the glittering blue ribbon that was the blessed Iteru, moonlight shining off her slow-moving waves.

The sight of the river lightened her spirits somewhat, but then they came crashing down when several hideous forms shambled into view, moving between the road and the river. The forms staggered and shuffled and made strange hollow sounds from the remains of their throats. Her mouth unhinged in a silent scream. The creatures were dressed in shabby, moldering linen strips, and looked for all the world like the justified dead risen from their tombs to walk the earth anew.

"But...that's impossible." And yet there they moved before her living eyes. She forced herself to focus on them, alternately tamping down a strong feeling of being sick and flinching at a fresh burst of unintelligible whispers in her mind.

Each of the creatures had a sort of unearthly greenish glow. She'd never seen anything like it before. One of them turned its partially caved-in head toward her and seemed to stare at her with eyes that glowed with a bright green fire.

She uttered a little shriek of surprise and fell back into the wagon, letting the flap close again. She held her breath for what seemed like forever, but the thing didn't move the flaps aside, didn't make any sound.

Maybe it hadn't seen her after all? She clung to that hope and silently repeated it, over and over.

 AUNY SHIFTED IN THE wagon and moved close enough to nudge her, making Ruia yelp in surprise. "What's wrong? What did you see?"

Ruia took two long breaths and tried to gather her senses. She blinked, then said, "There's another wagon out there with our people in it. Men are guarding it with guns. And..."

She wasn't sure how to describe it, but pushed forward as best she could. "And there are things walking around. Ugly dead things with...with glowing green eyes."

Nauny shuddered and hugged herself close. "Those were in the village too, grabbing people and hitting them. One of them hurt my da."

Ruia nodded absently as she rubbed the knot

on her head. "One of them knocked my ma to the ground." She glanced at the children, then at the closed flap at the front of the wagon. Another long, fearful cry sounded in the night, then was suddenly silenced by a gunshot that sent a shudder down her spine. The finality of that noise was what scared her the most.

The coarse laughter following the gunshot chilled her soul. Something deep within her, below her heart, maybe down into her immortal *ba*, started to harden. It was a strange feeling, as if she had lost something she didn't know she had.

She didn't know why they had been taken from the village or why any of her friends hadn't tried to escape, but she was going to do all she could to stay alive. There was no way she was going to let these terrible men hurt her.

Ruia said, "We're caught like stupid fish in this wagon. If we stay here, we're going to die." She wasn't entirely sure that was true, but it sure felt about right.

Nauny gave her a wide-eyed stare. "What are we going to do?"

Ruia covered Nauny's mouth with her hands. "Shhh!! If they hear us, they'll come after us for sure."

She held her hands over Nauny's mouth until

the girl nodded in understanding. Ruia dropped her hands to her lap. "You should come with me."

Nauny shook her head. "With those bad men and things out there?"

Ruia nodded. "Yeah, but we can be sneaky."

Nauny gave her a sour look. "You're better than anyone in the village at hiding, Ruia. You should go." She gave Ruia a little push toward the back of the wagon.

Ruia shook her head. "I'm not leaving you. We should go together."

Some of the children, roused awake by their talking, perked up and gathered around. A plaintive chorus of "Take us too!" and "What's happening?" sounded in the wagon.

Ruia lifted her hands to encourage them all to be quiet. "Hush, all of you! I don't know what's happening or where we can go."

Nauny nudged her again. "You're the oldest here, Ruia. Go and find help."

Ruia nodded distractedly as the welt on her head throbbed anew. "There are some adults in an open wagon a few steps away. I'll go to them first. They're not being guarded." Ruia paused and considered that, the glimmer of a dark thought forming in her mind. She shook it off and then stared at Nauny. "Promise me that if I don't come back, you'll all run if they come for you. Don't let them take you."

Little Khemi piped up, "But what can we do? We're so small!"

Ruia shushed her and patted the girl's bald head, raking a finger along her short sidelock. "Hush now, Khemi. I've seen you run faster than some of our horses. If the bad men come for you, you get out of the wagon and run. The Iteru is to the left, through the trees. Follow the river as far and as fast as you can."

Khemi gave her a big-eyed look and then nodded, wiping her tears away with a brave hand.

Ruia gave Nauny a final nod and then turned toward the back of the wagon. She crouched near the entrance as the voices buzzed anew in her mind. She shrugged them off, focusing on the camp around her.

The guards still stood around the other covered wagon and those strange shambling creatures ambled here and there. Without another word to the children behind her, she pushed opened the flap and slipped out of the wagon. She lowered herself to the hard-packed earth, flinching as her bare feet touched the cold ground.

She paused for just a moment to steel herself, then ran for the open wagon. She got there in several long-legged strides, and then crouched and crawled underneath it as fast and as quietly as she could. The ground under the wagon was muddy and cold and smelled foul. She glanced down but the light was poor here. It was muddier under the wagon than it was around the rest of the camp.

She looked around the wagon. None of the guards or any of those terrible creatures seemed to have noticed her movement. She lifted her mouth to the bottom of the wagon, and in a harsh whisper called out, "Hello? Hey, it's Ruia. I'm under the wagon."

There was no answer, not even a shift of weight on the wagon benches. She frowned, and tapped quietly on the wood slats making up the base of the wagon. "Hello? Can anyone hear me?"

The suspicion grew in her mind that maybe the adults weren't playing at being statues after all. With one more look around the camp, she crawled out from under the wagon and lifted herself up.

A long, stunned look at the closest adults confirmed her most desperate thoughts. They weren't playing at being statues—they were all dead.

"--they were all dead."

THE MOON HUNG BRIGHT in the sky, bright Khonsu staring down impassively, surrounded by thousands of pinpricks of starlight. Tjety kept Heker at a steady trot, following the trail Meret and the other bandits had left behind. Meret had at least one bullet in him, he was sure of that. He siphoned some of his fading reserves of *hekau* to push away the exhaustion bearing down on him, and felt the results take effect.

The spell was a stopgap measure at best—he knew he'd have to get some proper sleep eventually. For now, though, he pushed his exhaustion aside and focused on tracking down Meret and rescuing the villagers.

As he guided Heker along the trail, he wondered how far ahead the rest of the bandits and their prisoners were. Based on the tracks they left behind, they had at least two wagons. With forty villagers in tow, they couldn't be moving all that fast.

He shook his head in tired frustration. How much of a head start did they have on him? How long had Pashet and the others been at the village?

He paused from time to time to try and get a better sense of the tracks laid out before him, regretting not having paid more attention to Master Paheri, known as the best tracker the Rangers had ever produced. Tjety had always managed to show up for his training in less than ideal condition, and while he had no regrets about how he had spent the nights before, he still wished he had spent more time on the basics before getting thrown out into the field with the Rangers' headcloth on his head and iron on his hip.

He focused his *hekau* and examined the tracks. He'd been wrong before—there were actually three wagons—large, four-wheeled affairs, each pulled by two horses. Given the depth of the tracks, all of them had to be weighed down. The wagon tracks were easy enough to puzzle out but the horse prints were harder to interpret. He couldn't separate which horses were part of the caravan and which ones Meret had taken from the village during his escape.

He didn't expect an ambush from Meret. He figured the man, wounded, would want to ride quickly to meet up with his mates. There was safety in numbers and the Kekhmet frontier was not a place to be alone for any length of time.

He chuckled. "Unless you're just stupid or a Ranger. Right, Heker?"

Heker strung together a series of snorts as he trotted along the road. Tjety chose to interpret them as agreement, though knowing Heker, it was probably sarcasm.

Tjety glanced at the tracks again. The footprints, now, those had him baffled. There were a whole bunch of them. It wasn't clear if they had been made by shuffling feet, or people being dragged along, or something else, but something about those particular prints made the hackles on the back of his neck dance.

After another half-hour of steady trotting, Tjety pulled on the reins to give Heker a break and dismounted. He left Heker to free-graze along the river shore. He stretched his legs and then took a swig of water from a waterskin.

He moved over to some of the blurry tracks and knelt down. He splayed out his fingers above the tracks, careful not to touch them. He closed his eyes and reached out with his *hekau*, hoping to find some answers through his enhanced senses.

Some of the tracks were mundane, but some, especially the shuffling tracks, had a taint of darkling energy about them. His *hekau* flickered in time with his jigging hackles. He opened his eyes and sat back on his haunches.

Tjety mused on those feelings for a few long minutes. When no great insights struck him, he took a few deep breaths and watched the moonlight reflect silver off the river. He was tired. He indulged in the thought of setting up a picket line for Heker and spreading out his blanket near the river, but no. That bastard Meret was still out here somewhere, and those villagers surely had no one else to come to their rescue.

Fort Sekhmet wasn't that far away, but definitely too far for anyone there to have heard the commotion at the village. And being a border fortress, he doubted any of the soldiers would be out scouting. They'd be wrapped up inside their fort, snug behind their walls, with good beer, good food, and plenty of camp followers to fuck. They wouldn't give a damn about the frontier citizens they were supposed to be protecting. Useless army regulars.

Tjety clucked at Heker, who pricked his ears but kept his nose buried in the lush grass. In spite of the lingering anger in his heart and the exhaustion creeping in, he smiled and walked over to his trusted horse.

"Guess I'll have to pull you away from another meal, my friend. Life is so unfair sometimes, but we gotta get to work. Ain't what I had in mind when we left Asyut, but no other Ranger was dumb enough to get sent out here, so this one is up to us."

He vaulted up onto Heker's back and gathered up the reins, and pushed into a steady trot. They followed the trail for another solid hour, and then a large shape in the road ahead caused him to slow and then stop.

Wary, he cast out about the area with his *hekau*, but his weary senses didn't detect anyone or anything waiting in ambush. All the same, he pulled his pistol and held it at the ready as he gingerly nudged Heker ahead.

Tjety recognized the form in the road as the horse Meret had ridden out of the village. Tjety nudged Heker forward, but his mount held firm and pinned his ears back. Heker wobbled his head back and forth as if to suggest there was no way he was getting any closer.

Tjety sighed and dismounted. "I guess I can't blame you."

He moved toward the dead horse carefully, alert to anything untoward. It was still and silent, and had been in the road long enough that flies and other vermin had already gathered for a midnight feast.

Tjety glanced up. A dozen or more carrion birds wheeled high overhead. They'd seen the potential feast but hadn't yet descended to investigate. He suspected they were waiting to see what he and Heker were going to do; to determine if they were a threat to their meal.

"Oh mighty Nephthys, your creatures are free to do their cleansing work. My horse and I won't interfere." He moved closer to the dead horse and reached out a sandaled foot to nudge one of its stiff limbs, but the thing didn't budge.

He got a good look at the horse, flinching back a bit upon seeing the ruin of its head. The salty remains of dried sweat on its flanks and the mix of bloody froth and drool on the remains of its lower jaw told him part of the story. Meret must have ridden the horse near to death, switched mounts, and then shot this one dead in the road to put it out of its misery.

Tjety holstered his pistol and glanced up again. The carrion birds were being a little braver, having descended somewhat in the air, still wheeling. There were now perhaps two dozen, all waiting to see what was going to come of their meal.

Meret had left the horse's bridle behind, but had taken the saddle and any other gear that might have been strapped to it. Bridles were cheap, but good Hesso saddles were hard to come by. Few in Kekhmet could afford them. The Pharaoh's personal guard used them, and rumor had it that Pharaoh himself had a couple, but most people of Kekhmet didn't have a use for them. Even he and his fellow Rangers rode with little more than blankets and good bridles, although they had adopted the use of pistols and rifles, which the Hesso had brought to Kekhmet when they invaded the empire so long ago.

The missing saddle made him wonder if Meret and his allies were well-funded, and, if so, who was providing those funds.

Tjety stroked his stubbled chin as he stared at the dead horse, something nagging at him. He glanced toward the vegetation to the west that soon gave way to sloping sand dunes and piles of rough rocks. The rugged terrain might make for a useful hole to hide in. Or perhaps a decent ambush site.

Suspicious, Tjety again dropped his hand to rest on the juniper butt of his pistol and tapped his *hekau*. He studied the ground around the dead horse more closely.

A large pool of blood had gathered under and around the horse. A thin trickle followed the terrain's contours and into the tall grass edging the road. The ground here had good irrigation from the river just to the east.

Tjety cast about with his senses and his eyes, leaving Heker to stamp his foot impatiently in the road behind him. After another long minute or two of scanning, and another tap into his precious *hekau* reserves, he found what he was looking for on some of the old pave-stones. A few drops of blood, long dried and at first glance blending into the ground cover—far enough away from the horse's remains to suggest a different source.

"Son of a bitch. Gotcha." He was confident that he'd caught Meret with at least one bullet as he made his escape from the village, and these few drops of blood seemed to confirm the matter. He focused on the dens of rough rock, noting the nooks and crannies that could hide any number of creatures great and small...or even just one desperate and wounded cultist.

Tjety darted a glance at Heker and gave his mount a staying motion. He then drew his pistol and moved toward the entrance to the rocky den, opening his senses to the full, feeling the drain on the dregs of his *hekau*.

TJETY LINGERED AT THE entrance to the den, debating whether he should call out to Meret, or just go in and try to track the man down. If his guess was wrong and the bandit wasn't here, he'd just make a fool of himself, but if Meret was in the rugged terrain somewhere, then the effort might pay off.

His senses offered nothing but breezes moving through the rocky den and the flutter of wings from the wake of Nephthys's daughters overhead. His gut told him Meret was in that den. After one more glance at Heker, Tjety grimaced, cocked his pistol, and headed into the rough maze of rock and debris.

Parts of the den were wide enough to walk easily, though some areas required him to contort himself to get through closely-packed boulders. On one such tight fit, he left a couple inches of skin behind, and soon enough his leather greaves and bracers were marred by fresh gouges.

The path ahead opened slightly. A small bunch of homespun fabric, possibly Meret's plain headcloth, lay lumpy near one of the rocky walls. He cautiously moved toward it, senses wide open. It was a trap, he was sure of it, but sometimes all you could do was to spring it and…

The pile of fabric let out a strange muffled rattle as he approached. He leveled his pistol as he moved in. His senses a-tingle, he moved closer…

…and then ducked as a gunshot exploded somewhere nearby. The bullet creased the air just past his head.

"Shit!" Tjety yelled. That one was too close.

As the gunshot reverberated around the rock walls, the pile of cloth moved on its own accord. A massive hooded death-rattler revealed its thick form and terrible black and red banding. He'd seen snakes like it before, but this fucker was at least three times the size of his forearm.

He took an instinctive step backward, stumbling on the rough rocky ground. A second gunshot cracked out. "Fuck!" He howled out in pain and surprise as a bullet knifed through the meat of his right arm, sending out a spray of blood. He clutched at the wound with his free hand. Somehow he held onto his pistol. As if in response to his cry, the death-rattler rose up and up on its rippling coils, spreading open its massive crimson hood and baring its glistening fangs.

In a mix of shock and surprise, he fell backwards and put two frantic shots into the spawn of Apep, spattering broken scales and ichor onto the rock wall. His wounded gun arm shook from the effort.

Tjety rolled away from the convulsing thing even as it snapped its barbed tail in a dying gambit to take him with it. The barbs caught on the straps of his leather over-kilt and he counted his blessings that none of the poisoned barbs found his flesh. He switched his pistol to his left hand and awkwardly put two more shots into the fucking thing for good measure. His left wasn't near as good as his right when it came to shooting and sword-work, and a quick glance at his ruined right bicep suggested that his lack of off-hand training was going to be a problem real soon.

A third gunshot puffed dirt a mere hand-span away from his face. He rolled toward the closest cover, wincing as dirt and debris ground into his wounded arm.

He rolled right into a rocky outcropping pushing up through the rough ground. He lifted his head to try and seek out wherever Meret had hidden himself.

Sudden tremors rippled into the rocky den and then it was all he could do to keep his head down.

The ground under his belly shuddered, and a low, throaty rumble grew in resonance and volume, shaking the world around him. Brain and ears rattling, he tapped into the last of his *hekau* and cast about in alarm, wondering if Meret had set off some form of explosive. Hesso-made blasting sticks were hard to come by, particularly out on the frontier, but not impossible to find.

No, this had to be something else, judging from the syncopated jolts in his *hekau*, which jittered in time with the shaking ground. It felt like something darker and more sinister, but what, specifically, he couldn't hope to guess at.

Larger rocks crashed near his feet, and then the ground shook with another massive upheaval. Tjety curled up into a ball, legs pushed tight against his chest and his arms tucked over his head. As the tremors worsened, he closed his eyes and mumbled hasty prayers to Mayat and every other god and goddess he could think of for protection.

As the tremors convulsed the ground beneath him, loud groans sounded from the rock walls as they shifted and ground against each other.

Someone uttered a loud cry of pain through the cacophony, and Tjety wasn't sure if it had been Meret or himself. Clouds of dust and debris obscured everything, got into his lungs, and set him on a bout of severe coughing. He reached up with one shaking hand to unravel his headcloth and wrap it around his mouth and nose as a sort of makeshift filter.

An unearthly groan sounded from the depths of the earth, and he felt an unnatural chill deep within his *hekau*. The world around him gave one last, great heave, as if the earth were giving birth to a new moon. A shower of debris descended and then turned into a downpour that blocked out the waning moonlight. Rocks caromed off his back and his head and plunged him into sudden, utter darkness.

RUIA STARED AT THE bodies in the wagon, unable to fully comprehend what she was staring at. How could they be dead? All these people she knew from her village, all dead?

Gruff voices from beyond the wagon startled her out of her reverie and she looked around the small camp in panic. Two men were walking toward the wagon from a small tent at the edge of the camp, carrying her friend Yuti between them.

Her breath caught in her throat, a hundred moments of joy with Yuti flashing by. She leaped into the wagon and forced herself in and among the cold, stiff bodies.

She hunkered down and forced her breathing to slow. She clamped her hands over her mouth to try and stop the scream rising in her throat. If she wasn't silent now, she was going to die.

Harsh Hesso words filtered in, and the steps of the men crunched on the cold ground outside the wagon. The two men grunted, and then the remains of poor Yuti thudded onto the pile of bodies around her.

She tightened her hands over her mouth and squeezed her eyes shut, and willed her roiling thoughts to slow down, to be quiet and still. She reached down within herself for any scrap of calmness and coherence, and slowly built a cell in her mind to lock away her fear and despair.

Ruia breathed as quietly as she could and strained with all her might to listen to the two men. They made more Hesso talk with each other, which somehow sounded more familiar to her now even though she couldn't piece out the words. They laughed coarsely and then walked away from the wagon. She breathed fast through her nose, whistling slightly with every breath.

She sat like that for what felt like a thousand heartbeats, eyes clamped shut to the horrors pressed in around her. She heard a lot of cries from the wagon where she had left Nauny and the other children behind, and then the thud of feet on the ground. Someone was scampering away from the camp! Two Hesso voices shouted out, and then the air was split by the single crack from a long rifle. The running sounds stopped, replaced by a shuffle, and then there was a final thud of a body hitting the ground.

Her eyes snapped wide open and she muffled a scream into her hands. She heard it as a moan, and then clamped down again, hoping desperately that the bastards hadn't heard her.

A cry sounded from the children's wagon, answered by shouts from the guarded wagon where she assumed the village adults were being held. Then there was a lot of angry Hesso yelling, and a lot of thudding and banging around, and another gun shot, this one higher-pitched, like from a pistol. Things got quieter after that, and then she heard sandals on the ground crunching away again and more muffled Hesso talk.

She shook her head, the tears flowing freely from her eyes. There was nothing she could do. She was trapped in a wagon of the dead, waiting for her turn to die. Desperate, exhausted, and more afraid than she had ever been in her short sixteen years, she pulled her legs to her chest, wrapped her arms around herself, and just shook in the cold night. She retreated deep within her mind, seeking solace in a silence that soon changed to a form of companionable whispering sounding deep within her.

Confused, she focused on the whisperings. They had come and gone over the last couple days, though the realization struck her that she had actually started occasionally hearing them more than a year ago, around the time her childlike body had started to change over toward full womanhood.

The whispers slowly coalesced into a formal-sounding language that she hadn't heard before, though as she thought of it a memory snapped into place and she realized that she *had* heard it once, when she was born and the provincial priest had come to visit the village and offer her blessings on all the newborn babes and their parents. It was the heightened language of the priests and the nobles. No one in her village could speak it, not even old Elder Henutawy, who had seemed to know something about everything.

The elevated voice was soothing and calm, and in spite of all the terror around her, Ruia felt herself relax into the words, into the litany. An image formed in her mind's eye, a vague outline that soon slid into focus as a tall, regal woman with a perfect complexion and kohl-lined eyes, her whole body framed in a light blue nimbus. She carried a stern yet kindly expression and had a magnificent hawk's feather prominently arranged in the long plaits of her dark hair. Ruia had never seen a goddess before other than in an old scrap of papyrus Elder Henutawy had kept safe, and was certain that this gorgeous, glowing woman was divine.

As if in response to her thought, the vision before her offered the slightest nod of her head. The smile soon changed to a firm line, and then without moving her mouth, she somehow spoke into Ruia's mind. "Time grows short, fisherman's daughter." The words were kind yet firm, and Ruia found herself unable to resist hearing every word, spoken clearly in her language.

"You walk a difficult path, but there is strength within you. Look to my servants, and live forward rather than back."

Ruia nodded, unsure if the goddess would see. Of all the endless questions rolling around in her mind, she picked the most basic. "Who… who are you?"

The goddess said, "I am Mayat, the Lady of the

Judgment Hall, the One Who Guides. My eyes see all. And I see you, Ruia. Mark me, and remember. Go, now."

The bright form of Mayat faded from her mind's eye, leaving her in silence and darkness once again. However, the whispers in her mind altered to something more familiar and comforting, and she felt her hands reach up to clasp the simple lapis amulet hanging around her neck, the amulet that had been a birthday gift from her ma.

Ruia opened her eyes and focused on the amulet. The rounded piece of lapis lazuli had depth to it, and even in the poor moonlight filtering through the bodies packed around her, she could just barely see the outline of a single feather etched deep within the stone. A coincidence or trick of the light? Or a sign of the Lady Mayat?

A loud Hesso curse roused Ruia from her confusion. She jerked her head up and banged it against something cold and unyielding. She glanced up into the darkness and bit her lip to keep from crying out.

The mottled, unseeing face of Yuti stared back at her, a neat little hole lined with dark crusted blood in her left cheek. Ruia buried her face into the crook of her arm, trying desperately to quiet her sobbing.

Everywhere she looked was a dead person from her village. Yuti here, Ankhu there, good old kindly Henutawy over there, with her prettily embroidered shift torn open and a vicious stab wound gaping between her breasts. Some of the people had their eyes closed, their faces twisted in pain. Others gaped widely toward the Duat. Some seemed to stare right at her, as if they were silently pleading for relief or remembrance.

She shut her eyes and mind to all of them and sought solace within herself.

A knot of grief formed in her belly and started to crawl up her throat, but a cooling wave of calmness pulsed from somewhere deep within her *ba* and through the amulet in her hands. She forced herself to take some deep, relaxing breaths, and slowly she regained control of herself. She opened her eyes, steeled herself against the carnage around her, and wormed her way around the bodies so that she could get some sort of vantage point and look outside the wagon.

Three horses rode into the camp from what she thought was the west, their hooves clattering on the cold earth. One of the riders, a man with an ugly scar on his face, called out in harsh Hesso, and was answered by several of the bandits manning the camp. They didn't sound happy.

The scarred man, astride his sweat-stained horse, pointed at some of the other bandits and at the horrible creatures milling around near the camp. She wished she could understand what he was saying, and tried to focus on how he was acting rather than on what he was saying.

The whispers in her mind returned and the amulet around her neck pulsed softly, in time to the rise and fall of the voices. She rubbed absentmindedly at the bump on her head, which had cooled somewhat from earlier. She focused on the whispers and realized that through them she could make sense of the scarred man's words. As she made the connection, she felt something like a pulling from deep within her stomach, or somewhere just below it, as if she was channeling something of herself into the amulet and enabling the whispers in her mind to translate the ugly Hesso words.

The scarred man said, "What do you mean Meret stayed behind?"

Another bandit, one wearing a pretty necklace he

must have stolen from Mama Sitre, said, "You know Meret, boss. He got it in his mind to have a little fun with a few of them villagers. He kept Pashet and Uni with him."

Scar swore. "That useless sand-packer. Get this camp moving, Belko. Start back toward the quarry. Master Deshi's angry enough as it is at the delay. Don't make it any worse by dawdling."

Scar turned toward the wagon full of bodies. Ruia receded away from her vantage point and clamped her hands over her mouth again, hoping he hadn't seen her.

"Gods dammit. You were supposed to keep the prisoners alive. The Deshi needs living slaves, not a bunch of stupid, mindless laborers."

The bandit named Belko opened his mouth to speak, but Scar raised a hand in warning. "I don't want the details, Belko. Save your excuses for Master Deshi." He shook his head and then nudged his horse toward the edge of camp. He glanced to the east, toward the slow-rising sun peeking over the horizon. "Assuming they didn't spend the night in the village, Meret and the others can't be that far away—maybe a couple hour's ride. We'll go retrieve them."

He stared at the other bandits around him. "In the meantime, get these wagons moving. Roll as fast as you can toward the quarry, but set up camp if you don't think you can get there before moon-up."

Scar took one more look at the wagon of bodies, then rode to loom over Necklace-stealer, the man he'd called Belko. "And no more killings. Any of your men so much as touch one of the prisoners, you shoot that bastard and add him to the stack of dead. He'd be more use to us as a construct than a breathing soldier."

He gave Belko a long look then added, "Got it?"

Belko, looking sufficiently chastised, nodded and then turned his attention to the ground. Scar pulled his horse's head around and rode toward the edge of the camp, waving for his two silent companions to join him.

Ruia watched them ride off, silently praying thanks to the goddess Mayat that she hadn't been seen. After a long moment, she also added her thanks to Djehuti, scribe of the gods, for her newfound ability to understand the Hesso words. She shook her head, not sure what to make of it. Whatever the case, the whispers in her mind had quieted down again, and the strange pulling sensation from her stomach had eased. The feeling was replaced by one of surprising hunger, and her stomach lurched and roiled, reminding her that it had been nearly a day since she had last eaten.

She peeked out through the dead limbs of the adults and watched the men left behind start to break up the camp. A couple stood guard over the two covered wagons while the rest gathered supplies and readied horses. Two more muttered amongst themselves as they headed into the trees.

As she took in the state of the camp, she suddenly realized that she would have no better opportunity to make a run for it. All of the bandits in the camp were occupied with one task or another, and it would be much harder to make an escape once the caravan was underway.

Her mind racing with ideas, she cast her eyes around the cramped confines of the death wagon. She had to find something—there!

Poor dead Yuti was stretched out next to her, partially leaning up against Papa Intef's still form. Ruia steeled herself, then reached over and started unbuckling the girl's sandals. The cold, clammy flesh made her shiver, and she bit down on her lip to keep from making a noise.

Her hands shook with anger as she undid one buckle, then another. Yuti didn't deserve what had happened to her—none of them had. She'd find a way to strike back at these foul men.

But this sandal! It took some careful maneuvering and a little brute force to pull the sandals off Yuti, but once she had them in hand, it took her no time to buckle them onto her own feet.

She pushed her way through the bodies to the edge of the wagon, and paused in a mix of wonder and terror. Her da's body was wedged into one of the corners of the wagon, a couple other bodies perched on and around him.

Tears welled in her eyes as she took in his broken form, his strong arms that had once held her in comfortable hugs and the large, clever hands that had shown her how to bait a hook and gut a fish. He had a terrible bloody hole in his chest. His eyes were open and unfocused, his headcloth a mess of bloodstained fabric.

She stared at him in silence, her thoughts a mix of sorrow and vengeance. She leaned in close to him and rested her forehead against his cold, stubbled cheek, remembering better days when that cheek had been warm and full of laughter.

"Oh, da. What have they done to you? To all of us?" She focused on his face and lifted a hand to close his eyes, then with a flash of inspiration, gently unwound his headcloth and wrapped it loosely around her own neck. "I don't know how, but I'm going to get help and come back for you all, living and dead. I love you, da." She rested a hand over the ugly hole in his chest, and pretended for a moment that he was healthy and whole, and merely sleeping.

Then she took a deep breath and returned to her new reality. Her da and ma were dead, along with many of her fellow villagers. And yet many were still alive, prisoners of these foul men. It was time to run from this place, to get help.

She turned away from her father's body and looked out of the wagon, around her immediate area of the camp. Seeing no one focusing on the wagon, she marshaled her strength and leaped out. Her sandaled feet hit the cold ground and she ran as fast as she could toward the nearby trees.

She had nearly gained the cover of the trees when she heard a voice cry out to her left, close to the river.

Ruia didn't stop. She turned away from the voice and followed the river. Based on the direction of its flow, opposite to her movement, she knew she was moving generally southward. She breathed a sigh of relief. South was toward the fort, and far beyond that, her village.

More cries sounded from behind her, but she didn't dare slow to turn and look. She ducked down lower into the overgrowth among the trees, but kept moving.

Sounds from ahead stopped her in her tracks, and she crouched down to ground, finding a hollow in a tree to press against. She extended her hearing as far as she could. The voices ahead of her sounded really close.

She willed herself to calm down and controlled her breathing, feeling like she was getting used to being very quiet.

A man's voice sounded from nearby, in Hesso again. She focused on her amulet and on the whispers in her mind, and felt a pulling sensation in her gut once more. The words again became clear to her. "Was sure I'd heard something over here. Let's check it out."

Another voice responded, "Come on, we've got to get these things back to camp. Stupid idiots go wandering off by themselves at night."

The first one replied, "We should tie them up

like the mules that they are."

Ruia stayed crouched, even as the bushes near her rattled with the sound of their passing. They were just a few feet away.

"Here, I found the path. Let's get back to the camp."

Ruia risked rising up a bit on her haunches and peered through the thin foliage. Two rough bandits, dressed as the others in leathers and plain headcloths, had a long line of rope between them to which leads were tied to a trio of those ugly unliving creatures. The creatures made no voice as they shuffled through the bushes.

One of the men paused and scanned the trees around him. Ruia focused on hiding and kept silent. She felt another drain from within and wondered if it was somehow related to her lifelong talent at hiding. Questions rolled around in her mind but no answers came to her.

The man finished his scan, and, apparently satisfied, waved at the other man. They resumed their trudge through the bushes back toward the camp. She breathed a sigh of relief. She didn't understand what the whispers and the drain on her *ba* might mean. Perhaps it was divine Anubis helping out a lost soul, or perhaps just her imagination. She rubbed at the knot on her head. She had been hit pretty hard. Maybe she was just imagining things.

She glanced at the river through the trees. One thing she wasn't imagining was that she was free. Free to go where she wished and free from those awful creatures.

Images of the dead bodies she'd spent the night with sprang to mind, and she knew what she had to do. She had to find some way to save the rest of her friends. She couldn't count on Necklace-stealer to keep the word he'd given to Scar. It was all too likely that more of her friends would die, before they reached whatever quarry they were being taken to.

She had to find some way to save them all. She considered her meager prospects, then settled on the only real choice available to her. She'd run to Fort Sekhmet and beg the soldiers there for help. The captain and his men were occasional traders with the village, and she remembered that her village's elders had a decent relationship with the soldiers. But even if they didn't, she knew it was their job to protect the province's citizens from harm. She was sure they would help her rescue her villagers.

With that goal set firmly in mind, Ruia wrapped her father's headcloth around her aching head, bound up her braided sidelock, and then ran south along the river shore, hoping to reach the fort in time to save her people.

THE SUDDEN NEED TO breathe pulled Tjety out of the formless black. He convulsed on the ground, lungs tearing at his chest to fill. Taking a thick breath, he coughed up dust into the fabric still wrapped over his mouth and nose. All sense of time and place vanished. All he could do was curl up into a ball on the ground and try to find air, to cough and clear the grimy shit out of his lungs.

As he got his senses about him and a drew a few decent breaths, he felt the heat of the sun on one of his legs, the one not buried in debris. He shifted his body, skittering small piles of pebbles and sand. Clouds of dust eddied all around him as he groggily got to his feet.

Tjety waved his hands in front of his face, then hissed from a sudden sharp pain from the wound in his arm. He grimaced at the gunshot. It was oozy and caked with drying blood and grime. He carefully probed the wound with his free hand, wincing at the sensations. He considered himself somewhat fortunate—while the wound was in his stronger gun arm, the bullet had passed clean through the meat of the bicep and hadn't broken the bone. It might be salvageable. But, the wound was filthy and there was no telling what had gotten in there. He'd have to tend to it soon, before it turned foul.

He reached up with his good hand, pulled his headcloth off, and worked it into a makeshift sling. He carefully poked his wounded arm into it and tightened the knot. It wasn't ideal by any means, but it'd serve well enough until he could take the time to properly tend to the wound.

Slowly, gradually, the dust settled enough for him to make sense of the changed landscape. One whole wall of the rocky den had collapsed, leaving a large cleft that opened to the sand dunes beyond. The nook where he had entered the small clearing was choked with rubble and swirls of sand. In a large pile of rock that must have detached and slid off the rock face, a hand poked out, scratched, bloodied, and filthy.

Tjety's hand shot for his holster; but the sling fouled up the movement. He twisted his gun belt around so that his left hand could reach the holster, but found nothing inside it. He numbly recalled that his pistol had fallen out of his grasp at some point during the ground tremors. He checked for his khopesh and was gratified to feel it somehow still hanging from the scabbard tangled in his kilt. He drew it out of its scabbard with his good hand.

He shakily drew the blade and took a step toward where Meret lay buried, and realized he was dragging something behind him.

The death-rattler's broken form stretched out behind him, the sharp barbs contained in the tip of its tail hooked into his leather kiltings. He stomped a sandal onto the snake's body and made an awkward slash, severing the tail just above the rattle and the barbs. The snake's body slumped to the ground. Grayish ichor oozed out of the stump. He sheathed his khopesh and gingerly reached down to extricate the rattle, careful to avoid the still-glistening barbs. Even dead, the creature's poison would be lethal.

Disgusted, he tossed the rattle aside. He wiped his hand against his dirty tunic and then worked his way over to Meret. He grabbed Meret's wrist and pushed out with his weary senses for any signs of life. Blood pulsed thin and thready within Meret's arm. Tjety called out to him and pulled at the man's arm.

A muffled groan sounded from within the pile of rocks. Tjety stared at the man's hand. "Do I pull you out or leave you to rot?"

He mulled the question over, then shook his head. No, he had to get the man out and get some answers if he could. Leaving him buried here to die would be a waste of an opportunity. He reached down and shifted the rocks around Meret's body, working to free him from the rubble as best he could with one arm.

Meret mumbled in an incoherent mix of Kekhmetic and Hesso and a third strange tongue that was maybe something unique to his cult, or possibly a rough border dialect. Tjety's training had taught him that multiple dialects had developed throughout the fluid border between Hesso-held land and Kekhmet proper. The mix of Hesso and Kekhmet cultures and peoples had been inevitable. As it was, the blended dialect hadn't worked its way south to the capital. No Rangers he knew of could speak it.

After several minutes of concerted, exhausting effort clearing rock, Tjety grabbed hold of Meret's free arm and roughly pulled him out of the rock pile. The bandit let out a cry of pain.

Tjety dredged up some reserves of strength and pulled him to his feet, put his good arm around Meret's shoulders, and then half-carried, half-dragged him out of the broken den and toward the trader's road. Heker was nowhere in sight—probably had run for cover during the earthquake.

He whistled out for Heker as he reached the road, then deposited Meret onto the ground only slightly more gently than he might have otherwise. Meret stretched out, bleeding and coughing. He didn't look to be in any condition to offer resistance, but Tjety patted him down one-handed, just to be sure. He found a folding knife and a small leather satchel, and tossed them aside, several feet away.

Tjety glanced around the sunlit sand dunes and at the glittering river to the east, and mustered up the strength for two more concerted whistles. After a long quiet moment, he heard a whinny in response and then hooves hitting the dirt.

Heker jogged over one of the low hills between the road and the river and to him, fat droplets of water dripping from his mouth and nose. Tjety offered quick thanks to Mayat and then gave Heker a long rub along his neck, both to welcome him back but also to check for any wounds.

"Were you the smart one and went running when the ground started to shake?"

Heker nosed his chest in response, leaving a wet spot behind, then pricked his ears toward Meret as the man let out a low groan.

Tjety pulled a length of rope and a picket spike from the knapsack fastened to Heker's back. He hobbled Meret with the rope, who put up little complaint. It was probably an unnecessary gesture given his condition, but Tjety was inclined to be cautious. He shoved the picket spike into the ground some distance away and then tied the rope to it. He gave Heker an affectionate scratch on the flank. "Watch him. I'll be right back."

Heker gave him another snort that he fancied sounded like an affirmative. Tjety headed back to the remains of the rocky den. He wasn't about to leave his pistol behind.

Sunlight spilled over the rim of the shattered den as the morning form of the god Re made his way across the sky in his mighty sun chariot once again.

In a glint of light off metal, Tjety found his pistol almost straightaway, grip buried under debris but the barrel out of the ground and pointing toward the sky. Perhaps the gods were humoring him or taking pity. Or maybe he'd just gotten lucky.

He picked it up and turned it over. Somehow it had survived the quake, though there were new gouges in the juniper grips, and the chambers and hexagonal barrel were completely fouled with grime. He'd need to spend some time properly cleaning it—time he didn't have right now. He managed to holster his precious weapon left-handed and picked his way out of the rocks. He returned to Heker, who stood sentinel over Meret's prone form.

Tjety grimaced at the pain in his arm as he resettled it in the sling. He stared down at Meret. "What am I gonna do with you now, you son of a bitch?"

Meret opened his mouth as if to speak, then shut it and dropped his head back into the dirt. "Ya got me, Ranger." He wheezed, and turned his head to spit. He clenched at his thigh with both hands and groaned.

Tjety pulled his waterskin and medical kit off Heker's back and took a knee. He poked around in the satchel one-handed, scrounging for some bandages. He glanced at Meret. "If I go and get some water, promise you won't run off?"

Meret stared at him. "Fuck you." He feebly kicked out his hobbled feet. "You know I ain't going nowhere. 'Sides, ya shot me, bastard." Through gritted teeth, he muttered, "I'm afraid to stand up for fear of my leg falling off."

Tjety glanced at Meret's hands, clenched over his bloody and grimy kilt. "No less than you deserve. How many people did you kill in that village? How many more are suffering some other fate thanks to you?"

Meret shot a glance at him, then rolled over, pain etched on his face. Tjety stood up and made the short walk to the river. He knelt down and poured the contents of his waterskin over his head. He filled it, drank deeply, then filled it again. He sluiced water over his wound, regretting having drunk his medicinal alcohol. Should have kept it for what it was meant for. He'd remember that next time. He grit his teeth as he poured more water onto the wound, realizing that it was going to be a mighty struggle to clean it one-handed. He'd have to figure out the balancing act later.

He filled the waterskin once more and then limped back to Meret and Heker. Meret glanced up at him and then away, licking his crusty lips. Tjety leaned down and offered the waterskin. "Ain't much, but it's cold and wet."

Meret glanced up with hate glittering in his eyes. Tjety thought the man might slap the waterskin away. But, the bandit pulled one bloody hand away from his leg and accepted the waterskin. He gulped greedily from it, then handed it back, half-full. Tjety moved away from him and wearily took a seat on the ground nearby. He cradled the waterskin in the crook of his slung arm, and fished around in his medical satchel again.

He dug out a couple clean bandages, and, wetting them down, started to gingerly poke at the grime caked into his wound. He glanced at Meret as he worked. "Why attack a fishing village and take the people prisoner? What possible fucking use could they be to you?"

Meret rolled over onto his side so that he faced Tjety. "We got plans."

Tjety frowned at that. "And the sand is eternal. What kind of plans?"

Meret coughed around a hollow chuckle. "You'll find out soon enough."

"Not real helpful."

"Fuck you. You just gonna kill me anyway." Meret winced and pawed at his leg. "Assumin' this don't kill me first."

Tjety sluiced more water onto his arm. A thin rivulet of blood-tinged water trickled down his tattered sleeve. He was gonna have to burn the wound to save the arm. That meant making a fire, which meant taking more time he, and especially those villagers, just didn't have. Fuck.

He considered the problems before him, then asked, "How far ahead are the wagons and the rest of your people?"

Meret laid his head down on the ground. He whispered, "Fuck you, Ranger."

Tired of it all, Tjety barked at him, "Gods damn you, how far? Your *ba*'s already pretty shaky in the eyes of Lady Mayat. Do something to help me help those innocent villagers and maybe the dread Lord Osiris will judge you better than you deserve!"

The look in Meret's eyes suggested he saw right through his horseshit. Tjety didn't care. He asked again, "How far, Meret? A day? More?"

Meret closed his eyes and rested his head on the ground, mumbling to himself in Hesso.

Tjety pressed the wet compress to his wound and adjusted his makeshift sling to hold it in place. He stood up. He wasn't going to get anything more out of Meret. He had to get after that caravan. All he could do now for Meret was to send him on his way to the Duat. He dropped his hand to his pistol grip, then frowned. He hadn't had a chance to clean the thing. He'd have to use his khopesh. Left-handed. Shit.

As he drew his blade, he said, "I'd shoot you, Meret, but I have to resort to blade work instead. If you hold still, I promise I'll make it quick. It's a better death than making you linger over that gunshot."

Meret pushed himself up to a sitting position. His eyes were squinted tight against the rising sun. "Fuck you and your horse, Ranger. May you both lose your fuckin' way in the darkness on the last road."

Tjety didn't have a response for that. He limped behind Meret and raised his khopesh for the killing blow.

The sudden crack of a rifle reached his ears just as his blade spun out of his grip. He clutched his numbing hand to his chest as he staggered away from Meret in surprise. Heker started and wheeled away.

Three rough riders clad in dark leathers and headcloths as plain as Meret's loomed on the road ahead, spreading out in a grim row. The one in the center, sitting tall in the saddle, cradled a Hesso-made Wech carbine. The scar splitting his face was visible even at this distance. He cranked another round and then leveled the rifle.

In Kekhmetic much more polished than his looks, Scar said, "We'll take over from here, Meret. Seems you've gotten yourself into a bit of trouble."

Tjety glanced at Meret and then at Heker and his pinned ears. He returned his gaze to the brigands and their weaponry as they closed in on him. He winced at a new spike of pain from his wounded arm.

He just couldn't score a fucking break.

11

RUIA ALTERNATED JOGGING AND walking along the western shore of the Iteru, making what she hoped was good time. A couple times she ducked back into the tree line, thinking to avoid some of the thick patches of reeds poking out of the river along the shore. Crocodiles tended to lurk in there, and she had no desire to become an easy meal for one of Hapi's denizens.

She took breaks when her legs got tired, and drank handfuls from the Iteru when she could. 'Heat and lack of water can kill', she remembered her da telling her. She remembered the day her brother Paneb had gotten violently ill a few hours after getting home from a hunting expedition. He hadn't listened to da.

She especially remembered the vibrant yellow of the puke Paneb brought up. She had never forgotten the lesson. She was also careful to drink the water from what looked like clear areas of the river, and never drank downstream of a corpse.

Shortly before Re had ascended to high noon, Ruia took a break and sought solace in the shade of the trees lining the river. She wasn't entirely sure the tree line was any safer than sitting on the shoreline, but the canopy of trees and the foliage around her felt more secluded.

She took a few minutes to catch her breath and massage her sore legs. She wasn't used to running this much; all the more reason to drink a lot of water. The last thing she needed was to get cramped muscles, another lesson her poor brother had indirectly taught her.

Unbidden, Paneb's image appeared in her mind, young and vibrant and confident. He had been a hero to her and she worshiped all he stood for, even when he got away with things that she and her sisters never could, mostly because he was the oldest—not so much because he was a boy, though she knew that her da had doted on him a bit more than on his daughters. Ruia couldn't help but feel sad that her ma hadn't been able to provide him with more than one son, plus three daughters. He'd loved his daughters with all his heart, but she knew he had wanted more sons.

She thought about each member of her family then, recalling each of their faces clearly, as she had remembered them just before the attack on the village. She smiled at those memories, but they were soon supplanted by darker images of what had happened to them during the attack. Her father getting a gunshot to the chest, her mother getting bashed in the head and dragged toward their home. Her brother, brave Paneb, standing firm in the center of the street, swinging his hunting spear toward one of the bandits, but getting cut down by gunfire.

Of her two sisters, she didn't know what had happened to them. They were both younger than her, and should have been bathing in the river when the attack had come. Ruia furrowed her brow and tried to think back, for moments during the battle where she might have seen her sisters. Flashes of images struck her mind, of her father falling, screams ripping through the village, people running and crying, and the ugly bandit who had swung his rifle butt at her head.

But no memory of her sisters surfaced. She considered that, then focused on what she could remember from the wagon camp. Neither of her sisters had been in the covered wagon with her and Nauny, and she couldn't remember seeing either of them in the wagon filled with the dead.

She winced at that thought, then tried to bring up recollections of the bodies in the uncovered wagon. Several faces passed her mind's eye, the ones she was certain were in the wagon, the life in their eyes gone forever, their *bas* already on the long passage to the Duat. Her da...

No. It had been dark in the wagon, and she hadn't really been in the best frame of mind. All the other images of faces that appeared were blurry and indistinct in her memory.

That left the other covered wagon, the one that had been under guard, but she hadn't had a chance to look in that one. She had no idea how many of her villagers had survived, other than the few children that had been with her and Nauny in the first wagon.

She knelt over and bashed her fists against the ground as she yelled, letting out all her anger and frustration. She felt a pulse from her lapis amulet and a pull from her gut, and then stared at the ground. Somehow she had punched her hand down into the wet shore sand down to her elbow. Surprised, she pulled up with all her strength, getting her feet under her, and pulled her arm out. The ground made a wet sucking sound before giving up her arm.

She stared at the hole and at her arm in wonder for several seconds, wondering how in the glittering sun she had managed to do that.

A rustling in the brush nearby forced her mind to more immediate concerns. She stood and looked for a likely hiding place. There was a nearby tree to climb, and a couple thick bushes to climb into, but that was about it.

The rustling paused, and then without further warning, a large crocodile burst out of the bushes behind her and charged with a low rumbling growl.

She ran instinctively for the trees. She leaped up and caught hold of the lowest branches, and pulled herself up as best she could, her sandaled feet scrabbling on the lower bark of the tree. The crocodile snapped at her feet, thankfully just out of reach, and then circled around underneath her.

Her feet found purchase on the tree trunk, but it was a struggle to pull herself up and over the thick tree branch she had grabbed onto. She sought better purchase with her hands, but it was hard to find good leverage and also keep an eye on the terrifying beast below her.

A lowing from the river distracted her, and she turned her head to see a pair of young hippos emerge from the river and walk onto the shore, shaking water off their pelts.

As if things couldn't get worse! Ruia knew that hippos, when needed, could move deceptively fast and might very well catch her if they saw her.

"May all you gods give me strength!" She focused on her amulet to give her courage, and watched the crocodile move just under her. She pushed off the tree and landed on the crocodile's head with both sandaled feet, trying to drive all her modest weight down onto the creature's head.

It seemed to have the desired effect. The crocodile's mouth crashed into the ground, and she felt something give underneath her. She spared a quick glance toward the hippos and sprinted as fast as she could away from the beasts.

As before, she didn't look back, only focused on the path she was making. Turning around would just slow her down.

At one point she startled a ground nest of ducks, and they scattered around her feet. She nearly tripped on one of them, but maintained her footing and angled for the more open shoreline. Her feet fairly flew once she was on the shore, and she didn't stop running until a brutal stitch in her side forced her to come to a stuttering halt, her sandals splashing in the low tide.

Ruia bent over to catch her breath, and took the moment to look behind her. She saw waving trees, the lapping river on the shore, and her own footprints lined out behind her. No hippos and no crocodile. She clasped a hand around her amulet. "Thank you Mayat, and Hapi, and every other good god keeping your eyes out for me today."

She reached down for a couple handfuls of water, then knelt down and dunked her head into the river, letting the water wash over her stubbled head and sluice into her knotted sidelock. She put both hands on her sidelock and wrung out the worst of the water, then flipped it so that the thick braid hung over her right shoulder.

Ruia looked along the shoreline, not recognizing any of the terrain. Not surprising, since she had rarely ventured out of the village save for two trips to the fort with her da to trade goods, and one hunting jaunt with her brother that she wished she could forget.

She had run pretty far that morning, and had followed the river the whole time. The crossroads to the fort had to be somewhere ahead, which meant that the low bridge across the river at its narrowest point hereabouts would have to be getting nearer as well.

Unless...a sudden horrified thought struck her that maybe she had run along the river in the wrong direction. But, no, checking the current's flow assured her that she was going the right way. Somewhere ahead had to be the crossroads and the bridge.

She started to walk in that direction, then paused long enough to rummage around the tree line for a stout stick. After some trial and error, she found a likely candidate, and stripped a few small twigs and branches off of it. It was reasonably straight and felt solid in her hands.

She used it to dig in the dirt and eventually unearthed a few rocks, and searched around until she found one that had a little bit of an edge. She stripped the bark off one end of the stick as best she could, then whittled a makeshift point onto it. The results were less than spectacular, but it was better than being bare-handed.

Ruia examined the tip of her newly-made spear

and tossed the rock back into the underbrush. It would have to do.

If nothing else, she could poke the eye out of anything that came at her and then run like mad. She resumed her trek along the river shore, amused that her heart found newfound strength and courage from something so humble as a walking stick.

THROUGH THE BLOODY HAZE clouding his vision, Tjety realized that the scarred man and his allies were good at what they did; better than many professionals he'd encountered so far in his short life. As another solid punch connected, sending a spear of pain up his spine, the hope struck him that he'd be able to stretch out that life just a little while longer.

Another hammer blow fell on his shoulder, and he sagged to his knees once more. Through the stars twinkling his vision in spite of the bright sunlight, the blood-flecked ground underneath him rushed up and smashed him in the face. He sprawled out into the dirt. One of Scar's men giggled.

A hard kick to Tjety's ribs left him gasping for air, and then the bandit with the thick mustache kicked him onto his back and then ground a sandaled heel down onto the dirty bandages wrapped around his gunshot wound. Tjety howled from the pain.

"Lookee here, boss. Ranger got hisself popped." Mustache grinned brightly under that fearsome lip brush and leaned more of his weight into the heel-grinding.

Tjety cried out and then slapped at the man's sandaled foot with his good hand. Mustache was thrown off balance but somehow kept his other foot underneath him as he hopped away.

His lanky companion, the one with the ear-splitting giggle, stepped over and kneed Tjety under the chin. His teeth rattled. He crashed down onto his back again, sending up clouds of dust. He went for his pistol, but found nothing but leather and air where it should have been. He'd lost it early on when they had commenced the beating.

Giggles loomed over him. "You feckin' Ranger. Where's your fancy blade and your fancy gun now?" He giggled harshly and then stomped down on Tjety's left shin.

The hard leather greave strapped to his shin buckled under the blow but didn't crack. The thing had been crafted by the Rangers' best armorers. Tjety tucked his legs up and went fetal, trying to catch his breath but also desperately trying to keep an eye on his surroundings. These were the worst odds he'd ever faced and he didn't see any way out.

Scar was over by Meret, tending as best he could to the wounded man. Heker, poor Heker, had been roped, dragged down onto the trader's road, and trussed up good and tight. He didn't think the horse was badly wounded—if Scar knew anything about horses, he'd know that Heker would be worth a lot of deben, assuming he'd even sell such a fine mount.

Mustache and Giggles closed in, casting their shadows over Tjety. He squinted up through the stars in his vision and the pain all over his body, and coughed out some dust. He got another kick in the ribs and a piercing giggle in his ears for his trouble. He groaned at the new explosions of agony.

"Whatcha think we oughta do with him, boss?" asked Giggles.

Meret hissed through his teeth. "Good-for-nothing Ranger deserves to die."

Scar leveled a calculating gaze toward Tjety. "I suspect he certainly does deserve to die, and soon." Scar stood. "But we're not the ones to deliver that final act." He gestured toward his men. "Tie him up and get his horse fit to ride. We'll take them back to the quarry."

Meret growled in that weird border speech and slowly rose to his feet, staggering as he clutched at his thigh. "No, Qebsenuf! He needs to die, now. Gimme a gun and let me do him. Bastard shot me… it's only fair."

Qebsenuf, the bandit with the scar, rested a hand on Meret's shoulder. "Meret, you're weak and feverish. You're not thinking this through." Even through his pain-fog, Tjety caught the condescending tone.

"Our lord and master needs living slaves to complete the more detailed work that the constructs cannot manage. This one," he pointed toward Tjety, "will be more valuable alive than dead."

Tjety absorbed Qebsenuf's words, sensing something important contained within them, but understanding eluded him. Perhaps later, if there even *was* a later for him.

Meret gritted his teeth. "But I want him dead."

Qebsenuf made a sympathetic noise. "We all have wants, Meret. I wanted you to be stronger than this."

Meret met Qebsenuf's eyes, confusion and hurt plain on his face.

After a long silent moment, Qebsenuf added,

"Plead your case to Master Deshi. Perhaps he'll allow you to deliver the final blow." He gestured toward his allies. "Go, tie him up and get him onto his horse. We ride north to catch up with the caravan."

Giggles and Mustache each grabbed an arm and pulled Tjety to his feet, who winced in fresh pain. They somehow managed to hit every bruise and wound on his body. He dredged around for some strength in his *hekau*, but he was tapped out.

Exhausted and beaten, he was powerless to stop them from dragging him over to Heker's thrashing form. Giggles held him out of the way while Mustache laid into Heker with a short whip, yelling at the horse to be still.

Eventually, Giggles had to sit Tjety down on the ground with a hip-jarring push and lend a hand to Mustache. The two bandits managed to get Heker beaten into submission. Heartbroken, Tjety got a good look at Heker, who stared back at him with pain-glazed eyes.

Giggles tied Tjety's hands behind his back, sending up new flares of pain from his wounded arm. Then both he and Mustache lifted Tjety up and draped him over Heker's back, securing him fast with more rope slung under Heker's belly.

Meret shuffled his way over to the grass and retrieved his leather satchel and knife, and then fished Tjety's khopesh out of the dirt. "Maybe I'll use the Ranger's own blade to have a little fun, yeah?" He moved close to Tjety and spat into his face.

"Maybe take an ear for Master Deshi before we turn you into a slave, yeah?" Meret glanced toward Qebsenuf, and then leaned down and whispered into his ear. "Boss Qeb might want you alive, but there's a whole lotta hurtin' between livin' and dyin'." He shoved his knife into his belt and then flicked Tjety's face with the tip of his own khopesh. "That'll have to do for now. Later, I'll take me that ear."

Tjety felt the hot sting across his face, and then a warm ooze of blood slid down his cheek.

"That's enough, Meret." Qebsenuf wheeled his horse to stand near Heker. "I said I wanted him left alive."

Meret turned and uttered some Hesso curses, but backed away from Tjety and Heker.

Qebsenuf pulled Tjety's fouled pistol out from his waistband and tossed it to Meret. "Here, see if you can clean that up while we ride. It'll replace the one you lost and, who knows—maybe Master Deshi will let you use it to finish him."

Meret turned the pistol in his hand, examining

the dirt within it. Tjety squinted through the sunlight and pain and watched the bastard handle his precious weapon. He struggled against his bonds, but was just too weak. He offered a silent prayer to Mayat that he'd somehow find a way out of this mess before Meret turned that weapon on him.

At the end of his prayer, he felt a tingle in his *hekau* and, for just a moment, saw the clear image of a sturdy *djed* pillar haloed in a light blue glow. As it faded from view, hope sparked. The *djed* was a symbol of stability and strength, and its brief appearance suggested that maybe, just maybe, one of the gods was keeping a watchful eye on him.

Giggles led his horse over to Meret and Qebsenuf, and then gave Meret a hand getting into the saddle. Giggles said, "You're wounded. Take my horse. I'll ride double with Wendje."

Meret nodded his thanks, and picked up the reins in his free hand. He nudged the roan next to Heker and stared down at Tjety. "And you, ya feckin' Ranger. You're gonna take a nap."

Even with the warning, Tjety wasn't prepared for the thunderclap as he was pistol-whipped into sudden oblivion.

RUIA HURRIED ALONG THE shoreline, alternating splashing through the water with walking on the dry shore. She hadn't run into another crocodile or any more hippos, though she had seen a couple of the huge gray beasts sunning themselves on the far shore. She had also frightened a flock of geese into taking a honking flight away from her. Other than that, she hadn't seen another living creature.

Feeling that she had to be getting closer to the crossroads and the bridge, she took to the tree line more frequently, intent to see someone on the bridge before she herself was seen. She moved through the low brush and closely-packed trees, working her way around the river's bend. She crouched down when the rough wooden slats of the bridge came into view. This particular bridge had been standing for some years, and judging from the looks of it had weathered more than one small flood. She didn't know when the last flood had come through, though she remembered her da and some of the other elders muttering over dinner some weeks ago that the village was 'due for a good drenching'. The memory of that dinner made her sad.

Clattering hooves pulled her out of her recollection, and she instinctively ducked down to stay hidden. Along the trail on her side of the river, four horses came into view. Two had single riders, one had two riders on it, and the fourth had someone tied onto its back. She couldn't tell if the man was sleeping, dead, or something else. All the upright riders wore similar plain headcloths and riding leathers. She recognized the rider in the center as the man with the scar who had ridden out of the bandit camp earlier in the day.

Ruia frowned as she tried to remember the details. She didn't remember Scar's name, but knew that he had been the one giving orders and was the one the other bandits deferred to. The two riders doubled up on one horse were the same men Scar had ridden out with, and the other was slumped over and holding his hands to his bloody leg. That one she didn't recognize at first, but then his face flickered in her memory as the bandit who had been ordering men around the village. He was the one who had led the destruction of her village.

She tightened her grip on her spear, the rage building in her. She struggled against the urge to jump up and charge them all. She willed herself to focus on them. Frowning, she studied the man laying across the one horse's back. He looked different from the other four. A faint pulse from her amulet and a twinge from her stomach suggested that she should pay close attention to that one.

The bandits walked their horses over to the edge of the river and allowed them to drink and pull at some of the lush grass along the river's edge. She took the opportunity to carefully and quietly slip through the trees toward them.

She neared the edge of the tree line, where the crossroads to the bridge and the old trader's road leading north and south broke up, and hunkered down to examine the little party.

Scar got down off his horse and stretched out his legs, then walked over to the two men riding double and started talking to them. She heard the whispers in her mind again, and this time tried focusing on the pull of...something from her gut that fed into the amulet and allowed her to understand their words.

"Gods damn it, Meret," said Scar. "We are taking him back to the quarry. Let Master Deshi decide what to do with him. It's not up to us to execute him out here."

The one riding on the back of the doubled horse, the injured one, Meret, swore. "Damn you, Qebsenuf, you've got to let me do him now!" He spat out a wad of spit. Even from this distance, she could see the red-tinged foam.

Meret added, "I'm not sure I'm gonna make it back to the quarry." He turned angry, pleading eyes onto Scar, the man he'd called Qebsenuf. "Grant me my dying wish and let me kill that bastard."

Scar rested his hands on his saddle horn and shook his head. "You're such a whiny desert-dancer, Meret. You've been shot in the fucking leg. It's not like you've been gut-shot." He shook his head again. "I can't let you shoot him, Meret." He held Meret's gaze for a moment longer, then pulled a waterskin off his horse's back. "I'll get you some water. Anything else you want?"

Meret shook his head. "Just the water. I'm damned thirsty."

Qebsenuf handed Meret his waterskin, then pulled another one off his horse and walked over to the river's edge to refill it. Meret drank greedily from his waterskin and shot hateful stares alternately at Qebsenuf's back and at the man slumped over the other horse. Whoever he was, he'd made Meret really angry.

Ruia frowned as she watched and listened. The man lying on the horse looked like he'd been worked over pretty good. Bloody face, swollen lip, and what looked like a bloodstained bandage wrapped around his right arm. His arm sling was a long piece of fabric dyed a deep blue, and that sparked a glimmer of hope in her mind. It looked an awful lot like a headcloth, and only one group of people wore headcloths that color, though she had never seen one before—only heard stories about them.

A Ranger of Mayat? Her hand clenched around her amulet. Her brow furrowed. Mayat Rangers didn't roam this far north—they were only in the central area of the Empire and on the southern borders. Why would a Ranger be here, on the frontier?

She focused to get a closer look, but her eyes

hadn't deceived her—the sling was definitely the deep blue coloring of a Ranger headcloth. And none of the stories the elders had told about the Rangers ever suggested that someone would either steal a Ranger headcloth and wear it, or wear one without having earned it. The stories said that doing so would be to invite the righteous wrath of the gods and even Pharaoh himself.

She focused on the bandits. One of them had a fine curved khopesh strapped to his satchel that looked very out of place. The other bandits had straight knives and blades—what she'd expect to see on frontier soldiers and Hesso troops. It was the Kekhmet army and the Rangers that used the curved blades.

As Ruia puzzled over the situation in front of her, the sudden sensation of being watched tingled at her senses. Puzzled, she glanced around but then focused on the group ahead of her. The man laid out on the horse, the man she was certain was a Ranger, had lifted his head and was staring right at her!

She plastered herself to the ground, hiding in amongst the branches and fallen leaves and dirt. She reached out to pull a branch aside, too curious to look away. He was still staring in her direction, but not directly at her. His mouth moved slowly, breaking up the dirt and blood on his face, but she didn't hear a sound. That pleading look in his one unswollen eye told her all she needed to know.

Oh gods, what was she going to do?

AS RUIA STRUGGLED TO calm herself and her fearful thoughts, Scar refilled his waterskin and remounted his horse, then waved at his allies. "Enough of this. We have a caravan to catch up to. Let's ride."

He wheeled his horse around and nudged his horse's flanks with his heels, and started along the path, passing the bridge and heading in the direction of the caravan.

Ruia's eyes widened. What now? Wait for them to pass her by and then head for the fort? She considered it but shook her head. The Ranger could help her, could do something, and it seemed like he needed her help as much as she needed his. If she was going to act, she had to act now.

The riders moved close to her position in the

undergrowth. She stood up straight, pulled back, and with the whispers in her head sounding a warning, heaved her makeshift spear with all her strength toward one of the mounted men.

It struck a glancing blow on his chest and skittered off into the dirt beyond. He leaned hard on his horse's back, nearly falling off. He gathered his reins and cried out as he tried to regain his balance and control of his mount.

She stood there stupidly for a moment, only just realizing that she had thrown her only weapon away. And it hadn't been sharp enough or thrown hard enough to do any real damage. Her feet froze to the ground in her indecision. She gasped and tried to regain her breath, but nothing seemed to be working. Time slowed to a crawl.

Scar and his allies wheeled around to see what had happened to their ally, and then one of the riders mounted double drew his pistol and fired a wild shot toward her. One of the branches to her left shattered in an explosion of wooden fragments. She blinked dumbly, rooted to the spot. She was going to die right here, right now.

The man cocked his pistol for another shot, but then Scar hit his hand and the second shot went wild, lancing up into the branches far above her head. Her eyes grew wide.

"Don't shoot!" Scar yelled at his men. With those words, Ruia's world snapped back into regular time. She felt the heaviness shed off her legs, and ran as hard as she could toward the horse with the Ranger strapped to it. She scrambled in among the bandit's horses and managed to get a hand on one of the ropes holding the Ranger to the horse, but then a hand grabbed hold of her sidelock and pulled. She fell, spinning into the dirt.

"What do we have here?" asked one of the men. Somehow, her newfound ability to understand their words was still working.

Scar circled around to stand his horse between her and the Ranger. "Damned if I know. Any of you recognize her?"

The men shook their heads and made negative noises. Meret coughed and said, "Bitch's from the village, or the fort. There ain't no other settlements out here." He stared at her hard. "Nah, gotta be from the village. The only girls in the fort town are whores."

"I am no whore!" Ruia yelled.

Scar laughed, a harsh hollow sound. In her tongue,

he said, "There, Meret, you see? Not only a fisherman's daughter but she understands Hesso too! Quite the frontier maid." He wheeled his horse around and stared down at her. "You've got a lot of spirit, girl. I give you high marks for attacking four armed men with little more than a stick." He glanced at his men and then gave her a strange smile. "What in the lower depths of the Duat did you think you could accomplish?"

She fumed up at him. "You destroyed my village! I need the Ranger to help!"

His smile turned into an angry frown. "Bad answer." He motioned to one of his allies that had gotten in behind her. "You're coming with us."

The other man reached down and managed to get a hand under one of her arms. He pulled her up bodily onto his horse. She struggled as hard as she could, with no desire to be taken back to the caravan and that wagon of death.

Ruia cried out, but then the man shoved his hand into her mouth. She bit down as hard as she could and got a cuff on the side of her head for her trouble. Stars danced in her eyes. She bit down again, and got a strong punch across the side of the head, and then the arm around her waist moved up to encircle her neck.

"See how you like this, bitch." The arm tightened around her throat and she struggled as she felt her breath being taken away. She punched her hands against the arm and kicked the horse underneath her.

Soon, though, her vision started to swim, growing dark along the edges, and then she was struggling to get any breath in past the constricting passages in her throat. She croaked ineffectually, and her squirming and protestations slowed down.

Then, Ruia was hanging limp in the bandit's arms, just barely holding onto a thread of consciousness. Scar's head swam into view in front of her.

"Damn, she's got some life in her. Didn't know they bred them so hot out here. Hold her close and let's get moving. We're late enough already."

He moved back out of her line of sight and then the arm around her throat squeezed tight, like the one time she'd seen a snake suffocate its captured prey. The fog dappling at the edges of her consciousness swept in and over her, and plunged her into a deepening well of darkness.

JETY HAD LOST ALL sense of time and place. Sometimes he'd see trees bordering the road, and sometimes the Iteru shining in the sun. His battered body was subjected to constant shakes and bounces, none of which helped his aching head. He cracked open a swollen eye and found it hard to focus on any one particular landmark.

He tried to call to mind the face of the girl he'd seen hiding in the trees, but the constant jostling conspired to keep his senses muddled and his concentration uncertain. He tried tapping into his *hekau* for some measure of relief, but it was tapped out. He needed rest and food to replenish his *hekau*, and neither seemed likely to come to him any time soon.

His body felt like one big bruise, with added flares of pain from the gunshot in his arm and the cut on his cheek. Other than the girl he'd seen, the only glimmer of hope he had to hold onto was the brief image of the *djed* pillar he'd seen in his mind's eye before getting knocked unconscious again.

At some point during the seemingly endless ride, with the sun maybe an hour or two from setting, someone, probably Qebsenuf, called for a halt.

Tjety lifted his head and looked around. He was still stretched out on top of Heker, who was drenched in foamy sweat. Qebsenuf and his men had brought them near a small assembly of wagons, two covered and one uncovered. The covered wagons were guarded by armed bandits dressed much like the ones who had worked him over. The uncovered wagon was unattended, and a glance showed him why—it was clogged with unmoving bodies.

Why would the bandits have brought a wagon full of bodies? He puzzled that over, then a low groan nearby distracted him. One of the other bandits, Giggles, carefully dismounted his horse, balancing a groggy girl in his arms.

Something in Tjety's mind sparked, perhaps a glimmer of hope. It was the girl he'd seen in the trees along the trail. She had a bloodstained headcloth wrapped around her head in the same pattern as those of the villagers he'd laid out in the communal hall. Cuts and scrapes marred her face and arms, and she was filthy from head to toe—covered in dirt, dried blood, and bits of twig and leaves. She looked like she had rolled around in a series of fresh graves.

Mustache untied him and pulled him off Heker and onto his shoulder. To Qebsenuf he said, "I'll get this one squared away, Boss Qeb." He carried Tjety over to one of the covered wagons and heaved his body into the back of it.

Tjety hit the wagon's wood floor hard, and groaned. He managed to roll over to one side and cracked open his eyes to try and get his bearings. Several adult villagers sat dejectedly in the wagon. Each was dirty and looked tired, and showed signs of one sort of wound or another. They all looked beaten, defeated, and scared.

The closest villager, an older man, stared at him. "You ain't one of them brigands." He scooted closer to Tjety and gestured toward his tangled headcloth. "Dark blue? Are...are you one of them Mayat Rangers, son?"

Tjety met his eyes and nodded. "I am."

The old man's eyes widened as whispers of 'a Ranger!' 'here on the frontier?' echoed around the wagon.

"You here to rescue us from them bandits and their...things?"

Tjety frowned as the man's tone sent an unpleasant ripple through his *hekau*. "What things?"

The man indicated the opening of the covered wagon. "The dead reborn. The dead come to new life."

Tjety's frown deepened. "You ain't making sense. The dead can't walk."

Another villager piped up, wringing his hands. "But these can! May the gods preserve us!"

Tjety dragged himself to hands and knees and crawled over to the opening in the wagon's covering, looked outside, and blanched.

True to the villagers' comments, the dead did seem to be walking. A pair of mummified forms, gender uncertain, shuffled slowly along the perimeter of the camp, a strange sickly cloud of green essence surrounding them. Even without his *hekau*, he could sense their foul auras.

The things were unnatural, unliving creatures, constructed by some dark art well beyond his understanding. He'd never heard of such a thing. None of his training as a Ranger had even touched on being able to animate the dead. The very thought of profaning the justified dead in their final mortal repose was repulsive to his upbringing, an affront to every god, but especially the Lord Osiris.

What in the danky depths of the fucking Duat was happening on the frontier?

Tjety stared at the pair of foul creatures, absorbing what information he could. He scanned his eyes around what parts of the caravan he could see and picked out at least a dozen of the things, all of which shuffled along with no utterance or apparent intelligence. All of them looked to have been pulled out of ancient crypts or graves. Some were missing hands or even full arms, but all were mobile on two legs, or most of two legs.

He crawled back inside the wagon and glanced at the villagers. "These things attacked your village?"

Some of the villagers nodded. The older man spoke up again. "They don't move very fast, but they're stronger than they look. Between them and the bandits, there was nothing none of us could do. There ain't no way to kill them."

Another villager, an old crone, added, "The dead can't be killed."

Tjety rubbed distractedly as his arm wound throbbed anew. He suspected infection was slipping in. He sure hoped it didn't turn sour before he had a chance to put fire to it. That would be the only way to save it. He licked his dry lips with his dry tongue. "If these things can be created, they can be destroyed."

The old man shook his head. "We're not gonna to get the chance. They're gonna kill us all."

"I don't think so." Tjety raised one grimy finger. "If they were going to kill you, they would have done so in the village. Why bother dragging you all this way only to kill you?"

Yelling from outside distracted him and the others, and after footsteps neared the wagon, the flaps were thrown aside and the girl who'd been taken captive was tossed into the back of the wagon. She landed partly on Tjety and partly on the hard wooden planks.

She managed to work herself around into a sitting position and spit toward the bandit who had tossed her into the wagon. Mustache took the spittle full in the chest. He wiped it off, backhanded the girl back into the wagon, and then stormed off.

The girl wheezed a few moments as she tried to catch her breath. Tjety and another villager helped her to a sitting position.

Tjety stared at her. "You all right?"

She rubbed her head with her hands. "I think I'll be all right. Been hit in the head too many times lately."

He frowned at her. "Don't I remember seeing you in the trees?"

She stared at him and then her eyes got big and she nodded excitedly. "I saw you looking at me, and then something in my mind snapped and I knew I had to try and save you! You're a Ranger, right?"

Before Tjety could answer, one of the other villagers nudged the girl's arm. "My daughter! Have you seen Nauny?"

The other villagers in the wagon crowded in, questions and pleas piling on top of each other. The girl looked overwhelmed, and covered her head with her hands.

Tjety raised his good hand and called out, "Enough! Shush, people. Give her a minute to collect herself."

The girl gave him a grateful look and dropped her arms to wrap them around herself self-consciously. "I was in the other covered wagon with the children." She glanced at the worried mother and nodded. "Nauny is there, as are most of the other children from the village." She paused to catch her breath, and then added, "And I saw the bodies in the other wagon too, the uncovered one. It's…it's bad."

One of the elders reached out to her. "Who did you see in that wagon?"

The girl numbly glanced at him and then started to list names, but stopped after the third when Tjety rested his hand on her shoulder. "Stop, it's all right. Time enough to list and honor the dead later."

She trailed off and stared at him through tear-rimmed eyes.

To the group at large, Tjety said, "It's not so important right now who's alive and who ain't. There'll be time enough to lay your fallen family and friends to rest. For now, we have to figure out what's going on and what to do about it."

Some of the villagers still looked to be deep in despair, but some seemed to take his words to heart.

The girl stared at him. "Why did they attack my village and take us captive?"

Tjety thought hard on that one and dredged up memories of the recent past. "Their boss, the one with the scar, mentioned something about needing living slaves more than needing those walking dead things. Whatever these bandits are doing at their quarry, they need living people to do it."

"But what? Cut stone? Why take us prisoner to cut stone?"

The same questions rolled around in his head, but he didn't have an answer. "I don't know, but I'm sure there's a reason. They're not just out here to attack fishing villages. I'm sure there's a deeper purpose at work here. That's what we have to find out." The sound of movement outside the wagon distracted him again and he paused to see what was coming next.

Meret pushed open the wagon flaps and swept a glare across everyone in the wagon before resting his eyes on Tjety. "Boss told me to keep an eye on ya until we get to the quarry tomorrow. Wants you special, Ranger. Any of the rest of you cause a fuss…" He patted the grip of Tjety's pistol, tucked into the belt around his waist.

Tjety glared at the bandit and thought to make a move toward him, but didn't trust that he had the strength right now to make it effective. "Seems like your boss isn't too happy, Meret. Couldn't find something more important for you to do?"

Meret swore in Hesso and leaned into the wagon

enough to punch Tjety's leg. "Shut the fuck up!" Meret leaned against the back of the wagon. "Mouth off again and I'll put your iron to use."

Tjety rubbed at the newly-forming welt on his thigh. "I thought you just said your boss wanted us alive when we get to the quarry."

Meret grinned over clenched teeth. "He did, at that. But he didn't say shit about your wagon-mates." He pulled the pistol out of his belt, cocked it, then leveled it toward the girl. "Want I should blow this slut's head off?"

Some of the villagers gasped in alarm. The girl stared at the barrel with wide eyes.

Meret sneered. "That's within your power. Give me more grief and I'll pull this here trigger and send her off to the last road with your own gods-damned pistol." He met Tjety's eyes and yelled out, "Is that what you want?"

Tjety blinked a couple times, silently cursing himself for goading the man.

"Don't you let him kill me," whispered the girl.

Tjety stared at her, impressed at the grit in her voice and the flinty look in her eyes. If he hadn't been thinking straight, he might have been looking at and hearing his sister, Neferuta.

He peripherally sensed another half-dozen pairs of eyes in the wagon locked onto him. In a flash of insight, whether it was delivered from Mayat or something else, he realized he'd been a fool to focus on his own pain and misery. He recalled the oath he'd made in the village, realized he'd forgotten about it along the way.

Or had he just avoided it? He shook his head. Oh, dread Lady Mayat, please look kindly upon your weak-ass servant.

He took a deep breath that caught from the pains in his chest, and focused fully on the young woman. With as much conviction as he could muster, he said, "I will not."

He then turned all of his focus onto Meret. Digging deep for the right words and for any kind of support from his drained *hekau*, he said, "Meret, I apologize for what I said. Please don't shoot this girl; these people. If you've gotta kill someone, kill me." He spread his hands out in supplication.

The barrel of his pistol shook in Meret's hand. Meret stared at him for a long silent moment, and then leaned into the wagon again to shove the barrel against Tjety's forehead.

Through gritted teeth, Meret hissed, "Gimme

one good reason I shouldn't pull this trigger right here and now." His hand started shaking harder.

Tjety closed his eyes. "Do what you will." He braced himself for what he could only hope would be a sudden sharp pain and then a short trip to the Duat.

It didn't come, not after one long breath or another one. He cracked open one eye. Meret was staring at him down the barrel of his own pistol, holding the grip in both shaking hands.

"Gods damn you, Meret!" cried out someone outside of Tjety's view. Hands outside the wagon grabbed Meret around the arms and neck and bodily pulled him out of the wagon. His arms flung out wide and a wild shot from the pistol punched a hole in the wagon's canvas siding.

One of the other bandits dragged Meret to the ground while Qebsenuf glanced into the wagon with his scar livid on his face and then focused on Meret. "I fucking told you to guard them, not shoot them up! Get the fuck out of here and go get yourself cleaned up!"

Meret, sprawled out on the ground with a fellow bandit on his chest, blinked sweat out his eyes, and shot a look of anger and hate at Qebsenuf and then toward

Tjety. "This ain't the last you'll see of me, Ranger!"

Qebsenuf kicked Meret's leg. "Just shut up and be quiet. We'll be at the quarry soon enough. Maybe then you can kill him before me or Master Deshi decide to kill you." He gestured toward the other bandit. "Come on, let him up and go help him get cleaned up."

Qebsenuf shot another glare toward Tjety. "And you. I encourage you to also shut up and get some rest. You're gonna need it once we reach the quarry."

Qebsenuf turned and watched as Meret and the other bandit walked away from the wagon, then waved over a couple other armed bandits. "Watch they don't escape."

Tjety breathed a quiet sigh of relief as Qebsenuf moved out of sight, and nodded briefly to the girl. He sank back against the side of wagon and closed his eyes. How in the deepest pits of the Duat was he going to get the villagers out of this?

Meret and Qebsenuf were unwilling to kill him or the others, but why? Just who, or what, was waiting for them at the quarry?

He shook his head. He had no intention of finding out. Somehow, he was going to get them all away from this camp and from the madmen who'd taken them all.

RUIA RESTED IN THE wagon in a stupor after Scar left with Meret and the other bandits, conserving her strength and willing her throbbing head to subside. As the light outside transitioned from sunset to moonrise, her stomach growled from not having had anything to eat for well over a day. She was cold, tired, hungry, and unhappy at being stuck in a wagon again.

A nudge roused her. Elder Sefer leaned in close. "That Ranger wants to talk to you."

Hope sparked in her heart and she felt a strange little pulse from her amulet. She got up to hands and knees as quietly as she could, and clambered over some of the adults in order to make her way to the far side of the wagon, where the Ranger sat with his back pressed against the low wooden wall where the canvas top was lashed down.

He nodded at her as she scooted across the wooden planks and wedged herself in between him and old Ma Djedefa, who was snoring up a storm with her head lolling against the floor.

The Ranger put his good arm around her and pulled her in close, startling her. Her breath caught. What were his intentions? He leaned his head down and brought his lips to her ears. The scruff on his chin scratched at her earlobe. "We gotta figure a way to get out of here."

Ruia nodded against his mouth and tried to cover a shiver of surprise. The Ranger was talking to her as if she was an equal. "I agree, but how?"

"Not sure, but I'm gonna need your help. Maybe your people too."

A little jolt went down her spine and she felt the hairs on her arms stand up on end. Her people? What did he think she was, a village elder? She still had her sidelock of youth.

He added, "If we can get our hands on some guns, maybe my pistol, we might stand a chance. We can't all sneak out of here unseen. We'll have to fight."

Ruia stared at him in the dim light, a mix of

wonder and confusion rolling around her mind. A sudden thought struck her and in spite of the situation, she chuckled.

The Ranger asked, "What's so funny?"

"I know that bandit's name is Meret, but I don't know yours." She lifted her head to stare into his eyes. "My name is Ruia."

He smiled in the darkness, his teeth a break of white in the dim light. "It's a right honor to meet you, Ruia. I'm Tjety. I'm a Ranger of Mayat."

She returned the smile and tried to tamp down her excitement. "I knew it! When I saw you on the back of that horse, I saw your blue headcloth and your curved blade. I figured you had to be either a Ranger or someone who had killed a Ranger and stolen his things." She stopped herself short, realizing she was babbling. Gods! Why would a Ranger get her so flustered? She'd never met one before.

His body shook once as he let out a short laugh. "Nah, I haven't had my stuff stolen from me yet. Well, except now, maybe." He nudged his chin toward the wagon flaps. "Meret's got my pistol, and one of the other bastards has my blade. And my horse, come to think of it." He scratched at the thin stubble on his chin and sighed again.

She recalled the horse he'd been tied to. "I saw him taken to be with the other horses. I think he's still all right."

"That's good to know. I'm rather fond of that horse."

Ruia smiled at him, then shook her head, realizing she was mooning over him like a silly little girl. She cleared her throat and said, "Lady Mayat told me to keep an eye out for her servant. I guess she meant you."

He flinched hard against her. In a harsh whisper, he asked, "The fuck did you just say?"

She leaned away from his hold around her, tamping down a flutter of panic in her stomach. "I…I said the Lady Mayat…"

Tjety leaned in close. "The Lady Mayat…*spoke* to you?"

She nodded with wide eyes. "I think so. She said that's who she was. I…I got hit on the head, though, so I might have just imagined it."

He opened his mouth, closed it, then closed his eyes and took a deep breath. "How about you tell me everything that happened involving this Lady Mayat?"

Ruia blinked a couple times, then organized her scattered thoughts. "I was hiding in that wagon of the dead. I felt lost." She stared past him and beyond the open flaps of the tents, catching sight of a few stars in the night sky.

"I was so scared, and alone. And then I heard whispers, sort of, in my head." She glanced at him to see if he'd say she was crazy, but he was staring at her close, and she could feel the tension in his body pressed against hers.

"And I clutched the amulet my ma gave to me, and then this vision of a beautiful glowing woman appeared in my head, and she had long black hair and a large white feather tied into her braids."

Tjety let out a slow breath. "Lady Mayat."

Ruia nodded. "That's who she said she was."

Tjety shook her, insistent but gentle. "What else did she say?"

Ruia frowned. "She said something about a difficult path before me, to look for her servants, and something about marking her and remembering."

"Huh." He cleared his throat, and turned away to look outside, maybe toward the same stars she had seen. "Lady Mayat." He turned his focus back to her. "May I see this amulet of yours, Ruia?"

She nodded, and fished it out from underneath

the neckline of her dress. She cupped it in her hands and presented it to him.

He leaned in close and reached his wounded hand out of his sling and touched it. She felt a pulse from the amulet and another flutter in her gut. What had he just done?

He must have felt her flinch because he pulled his hand away and tucked it back into the sling. "By the Gods, Ruia, I wish we had more time."

She frowned and tucked the amulet back beneath her tattered dress. "Why? Time for what?"

He leaned his head back against the canvas and sighed again. "If that amulet is what I think it is, and if my weak and weary *hekau* isn't wrong, you're a very special young woman."

She shook her head. "I don't understand."

He squeezed her in a brief hug. "May the gods grant us the time for me to try and explain. For now…I think we have a more immediate issue."

She frowned again, feeling a surge of frustration well up inside her. "Don't you think for an instant that I'm going to let you forget about this. I want to know everything you're not telling me."

He smiled at her in the darkness. "I like your spirit, Ruia, and I promise to tell you as much as I can, assuming we get the fuck out of here in one piece."

Ruia sighed and also leaned back against the wagon's canvas wall. "Anyways, on that. Any idea on how we're gonna get some weapons?"

He nodded. "Once I got settled in the wagon, and once I figured the guards were gonna leave us alone, I got to work loosening the lashings to this wagon's canvas cover. I've got part of the bindings loose, but not enough for me to slip through. You're about half my size, so I thought you might be able to slip through the gap between the cover and the wagon."

She moved her hands behind him and pushed against the canvas. Sure enough, there was some give. "I think I can fit, yeah, but what then? Where am I supposed to go?"

He shrugged. "I figured you could check out the camp, get a sense of where things are, then come back and tell us. And then maybe we can rush the guards outside, grab their guns, and make a fight of it."

She nodded, a bit dubious, but was encouraged to be thinking of something other than doing nothing. She nodded, then pushed herself up to a crouching position. "I don't know about you, but I'm about ready to get out of this damn wagon."

He nodded. "Let's go for it, then."

She maneuvered around him and shoved her legs into the space he had created between the wagon wall and the canvas, and then slid her body partway down the side of the wagon. She held herself in place with her weary arms and turned to face him. "So I'll sneak around the camp, see what I can see, then I'll come back."

"Think you can get around the camp unseen?"

She nodded. "I'm good at not being seen. How long should I check out the camp before coming back?"

"How about to the count of a hundred? A slow count. Or until you see something important enough to come back and tell me."

She nodded again. "All right. How do you want to handle the guards?"

"While you're out scouting, I'm gonna talk to your fellow villagers here and ask them to help me rush the guards after you come back. I figure the lot of us working together should be able to wrest the guns out of their hands and then raise a fuss."

"And while you're raising a fuss, the rest of us run for the trees?"

"Something like that. Depends on how many guards are out there...and how many of those... unliving things there are." He rested his hand on hers. "If you're able to, try to get a count of how many of each are out there. It'll help me figure out whether it'll be better to run, or stand and fight."

At his last comment, her breath caught in her throat. She was sure there'd be too many of them. "If we try to fight our way out, we might all die."

He nodded. "That's right, Ruia. And if we sit here in the wagon and let them take us to that quarry of theirs, we'll probably die too. I don't know about you, but I'd rather choose how I die if I can. If I'm gonna die tonight, it's gonna be in the service of helping you and your people."

Her heart skipped a beat at that. She wished she could see his face in the darkness, but it was just a dark blur. She reached up and gently pressed a palm against his cheek.

"You're an inspiration, Ranger. Thank you." She flexed herself and got ready to drop onto the ground. "Wish me luck."

He nodded. "May the good gods walk with you and keep you safe, Ruia. To a hundred."

She gave him one last nod and then dropped

through the gap he had created.

Ruia tried counting in her head. She hit the ground with both sandaled feet, landing harder than she had expected. She crouched under the wagon and paused for several counts, waiting to see if anyone had heard her. Her vision adjusted to the change in light outside the wagon, and she wondered if maybe the good night-vision she always seemed to have was somehow connected to her *hekau*. She'd have to ask the Ranger.

She focused on the camp again. There was no movement save for the sound of some shuffling along the perimeter beyond. Must be some of those awful creatures out there.

She scanned the camp. The uncovered wagon with its grisly cargo was over to her left, while the other covered wagon was just ahead. Two guards chatted quietly in front of that wagon, and a quick glance showed two more standing near the back of the wagon she'd just jumped out of, sharing a smoke and passing a metal flask back and forth. Meret sat on the ground near the dying campfire, muttering to himself.

Ruia shivered underneath the wagon. A wet chill had gotten into the air during the night. The thin dress she had on was hardly sufficient clothing.

The uncovered wagon was about eight or nine strides from her wagon. She glanced around and then made a run for it.

Her count got to twenty by the time she ducked under the wagon. Breathing hard but trying to be quiet, she scanned the camp from this new vantage point.

She counted six men, including Qebsenuf, inside a large tent at the edge of camp, asleep in bedrolls or blankets. They had their weapons and other supplies stacked to one side.

The horses were just beyond the tent, all lined up, tied to a picket line made of rope stretched across a couple stout trees. They had a little room to graze, though most of them were dozing where they stood. The tall horse Tjety had been tied to was among them, looking healthy enough.

She had lost count, but started again at sixty, just to pick a number to go with. She hoped that Tjety and the others waited until she got back.

Footsteps near her froze her to the ground. She stopped breathing and put her hand over her mouth to help prevent any sound from coming, but also to help break up the mist of her breath on the cold air. She realized that if she breathed too heavily, the plume of frozen air might give her away.

The two guards from the children's wagon moved toward the tent with the sleeping bandits. They were talking in Hesso, so she pulled at her *ba* and felt the familiar pulse in her amulet. Their words became familiar to her once again.

"Can't wait to get back to the damn quarry. Betcha that cook's got a fine breakfast laid out for us."

"Shit. We'll be lucky to not become breakfast ourselves. Meret's really fucked things up this time. When Boss Qeb has to come all the way out here to shepherd us home, I don't expect good things when we get back."

"Hadn't thought of that. Shit."

They trailed off as they moved out of her earshot. Guessing her count had gotten close to a hundred, and feeling like she had seen all she needed to see, she got ready to run back to the covered wagon.

A shuffling sound in the woods nearby froze her, and then she remembered she had only counted half of their enemy. There were eleven bandits including Meret, but there were also those unliving creatures out there. She squinted into the darkness and tried to find the source of those shuffling noises in the scrub brush. The scattered moonlight filtering in through the clouds showed her possible shadows in the trees that were vaguely man-shaped, but not well enough for her to get anything resembling a reliable count.

She sighed in frustration. There were a lot of enemies for the Ranger and her people to take on, and most of the villagers were wounded, as well. She needed to give them a better chance—if they were to rush the guards now, they'd get hurt or killed before they had the chance to fight back.

Her mind racing, she used her vantage point to study the camp, a vague idea taking hold. Before she had a chance to second-guess herself, she ran for the picket line and hurriedly untied it, releasing the horses. She pulled the long rope out of their leads and dropped it to the ground. Most of the horses just stared at her, but the more energetic ones tossed their heads, seemed to realize they were free, and then started to wander off.

A quick glance showed her she was as yet undetected, so she scampered over to the tent where the six bandits slept and pulled a couple of the tent spikes, collapsing one side of the tent onto their slumbering forms. She then ran as hard as she could for the covered wagon to tell the Ranger what she had done, the bandits behind her starting to react to her distraction.

TJETY WATCHED RUIA DROP to the ground underneath the wagon. He shot a quick silent prayer to Mayat to keep an eye on the girl. She was full of surprises and he was confident he hadn't seen the full extent.

He started to count silently, and quietly moved toward the cluster of villagers.

He cleared his throat then nudged the villagers to get their attention. "Listen up. I sent Ruia out to scout around a bit."

The group of adults murmured in objection and concern. Tjety held up his good hand.

"Quiet! We can't afford the guards hearing us. Ruia's going to look around the camp and then come back and tell us what she saw."

One of the villagers leaned over and in a harsh

whisper asked, "Why would you send her out alone, Ranger?"

Tjety stared in his direction, unable to make out his face in the darkness. "Because she's smaller than me and was able to fit through the gap between the wagon and the canvas. She also said she's good at hiding."

Another villager, a woman, asked, "What are we going to do?"

"We're going to wait for Ruia to come back with her information, and then we're going to rush out of this wagon together and try to overpower the guards." He waved toward the back of the wagon. "I figure the only way out of this is to fight. Then we run for Fort Sekhmet. These bandits have friends at this quarry, and I'm willing to bet that there are enough of them that going back to the village would be a waste of time."

An old lady cried out, "But that's our home!"

Tjety shook his head. "Your home ain't safe any more." He paused, then added, "The bandits didn't leave anyone alive."

Horrified gasps and quiet sobs answered his dire statement. Hating to add to it but knowing that they had to know the truth, he continued. "I got to your village just as Meret and his two allies were finishing up. I killed two of them and shot Meret, but they had already killed seven of your people."

He got more sobs as response. Then, one of the men gripped Tjety's good arm in his beefy hand. "Tell us what we gotta do to make these men pay for what they done."

Tjety took that man's hand in his and squeezed it gently. "I say give them frontier justice. That's how to balance the scales."

Some nods greeted his words then, and some sniffles and coughs. The man said, "Just tell us what to do, Ranger. We're with you."

Tjety nodded, then realized he had lost count somewhere along the way. Running feet on the dirt sounded then, and then there was a thud underneath the wagon. Tjety got down on his knees and pressed his ear to the wooden floor of the wagon.

"Ruia?" he asked in a harsh whisper.

"It's me!" she replied, her voice muffled through the wood.

"What did you see?"

She cleared her throat. "There are eleven bandits total, including six in a tent that I just collapsed." After a pause, she whispered, "Sorry. It seemed like the right thing to do."

Tjety stared at the floor of the wagon as a commotion started to stir in the camp, as if the girl had whacked a hornet's nest with a stick. "Shit, girl! You were just supposed to scout around." He had to admit he was impressed.

Thinking fast, he got his feet under him. "Shit. This is it—no more time for talk. For your family and your friends, fight to live!" He faced down toward the floor. "Ruia! Do what you can!"

Tjety turned toward the back of the wagon and made a run for it, some of the villagers stumbling in behind him. He hit the ground running, caught sight of Meret standing near a campfire, and rushed in a straight line toward him.

To his credit, Meret jerked his head up at the sound of approaching footsteps, but was too slow to prevent Tjety from crashing into him, the momentum throwing both of them onto the hard dirt.

Tjety rolled on top of Meret and wrestled with him one-handed for control of his pistol. Meret's finger convulsed on the trigger. The shot went wild, the thunderclap shaking the night.

Some of the villagers stumbled out of the wagon and rushed the other guards. The air soon filled with shouts and gun shots. Cries rose up from the other covered wagon, and as Tjety wrestled with Meret for control of the pistol, Tjety caught sight of Ruia pulling children out of that wagon.

Meret bit down hard on Tjety's wrist. Tjety in turn, butted Meret with the hard part of his forehead. Back and forth they traded blows, at some point getting their feet underneath them and standing. Tjety tried to take the advantage by stomping on Meret's foot, and Meret countered with a badly-aimed kick to Tjety's groin. He caught it high on his thigh, and winced at the new knot of pain blossoming on his body.

In a surge of anger, Tjety pried the pistol out of Meret's hand, reversed the gun in his grip, and shot a hole through Meret's neck.

Meret stumbled back, both hands pressed to his throat, gurgling blood as he went down.

Tjety flipped the pistol around to the proper grip and finished the bandit off with a shot between the eyes. He didn't even watch Meret hit the ground. He was too busy turning to take aim at another bandit who had a rifle raised to shoot. Tjety's bullet took him full in the chest while the bandit's own hasty rifle shot went wide.

Another rifle shot cracked into the night, but before

Tjety could take aim, several villagers overwhelmed that guard, dragging him to the ground in a swarm of flying hands, feet, and yells of vengeance.

Tjety glanced across the camp. The men in the collapsed tent were pulling themselves together, going for weapons, and calling out to each other. And beyond them, the horses were panicking, and bolting in every which direction.

Across the camp that had become a confused battlefield, Tjety called out. "Ruia! The horses, get to the horses!" She turned to face him, the look on her face clear that she hadn't heard him. She had a young girl in her arms and a young boy's hand in hers.

He ducked down next to the covered wagon and waved at her to get her attention, then pointed toward the horses. "The horses!"

She looked in that direction and then back to him, and nodded. She yelled something into the wagon, got the two children loaded into it, and then ran at a fast crouch toward the picket line.

Then the other bandits with their weapons joined the fray and it was all he could do to keep sane in the ensuing melee. Bullets flew every which way, plowed into the ground, the trees, the wagons, and into flesh both alive and unliving with indifferent brutality. Horses cried out and charged around the camp or away from it, adding their own confusion to the chaos.

Tjety ducked under the closest wagon and fired his pistol until the hammer dropped on an empty shell. He shoved the pistol into his holster then reached out and grabbed a running sandal, knocking a bandit onto his back. Before the man could react, Tjety was on him. He battered the man into submission and then scrambled for that man's fallen pistol. Tjety rolled out of the way just as another bandit stabbed downward with a curved blade that looked terribly familiar.

Tjety came out of the roll firing, and the bandit stumbled back, new holes in his chest bubbling up blood. The man sat down hard on the ground, staring at him with dimming eyes. His khopesh fell to the ground with a clatter.

Tjety had just enough time to trade the empty pistol for his blade before the treeline exploded with a burst of shambling forms, their horrific auras outlined in a dank green fog, their bright green eyes nearly as bright as the stars.

He raised his khopesh high, cried out a challenge,

and ran for the creatures. He laid into them with his blade, finding them surprisingly easy to wound. The things weren't very fast nor very agile, and all they had to attack him with was brute strength and arms and teeth. Which, actually, was more than he could handle.

Tjety soon found himself surrounded by several grasping creatures, and flailed around with his khopesh and his wounded arm. He lopped off the arm of one creature and then another grabbed his leg and pulled, nearly knocking him over. That one's head suddenly exploded as Tjety heard the sharp report of a rifle.

He turned to look, and saw three villagers aiming his way with borrowed rifles. He cried out to them to shoot and dropped to the ground. The villagers opened up a withering array of gun fire. He covered his head and hoped their aim was sound.

The creatures dropped all around him, and yet some crawled toward him or toward the villagers. He grabbed one by the ankles and swung his khopesh into its back, cutting its spine. It opened its mouth in a silent scream, trying to clutch at the blade. He wrenched the blade out of the thing's back and glanced down into its chest cavity, which

"Tjety soon found himself surrounded by several grasping creatures..."

was glowing with a strange green light. He reached in and pulled out a small heart-shaped scarab, the source of the green glow. As soon as he pulled it out of the creature's chest, the moldy form suddenly slumped to the ground and stopped moving.

He stared at the scarab in his hands in confusion, watching as the green glow it emanated slowly faded to darkness. Somehow the scarab was the key to their unnatural life. He glanced toward the villagers, who were gunning down the last of the creatures.

"Shoot their chests! Shoot the green amulets in their chests!"

A couple of the villagers nodded in understanding and worked their way toward the last few mummified forms. Tjety got to his feet and then felt Ruia crash into him, breathless.

Tjety said, "Get your people into the trees and help them find cover! I'll get the last of the creatures!"

In response, Ruia said, "I didn't rescue you only to be thrown aside! Let me help you!"

"Help yourself and your people!" Tjety pushed her toward the trees, but then had to turn and ready his khopesh again to defend himself against another unliving creature shambling toward him.

He made short work of the construct with his

blade, though it managed to score a ringing blow on his already-wounded arm. He cried out in pain and then shoved his khopesh into its chest and cut out its green scarab. It fell to the ground without another swing.

Ruia threw her arm around him and helped him back toward the wagons. He cast his eyes all around, but it appeared that the battle was coming to an end. The odd gunshot rang out here and there, and the groans of pain from the survivors filled the night air.

He put a hand onto the closest wagon for balance, and turned to Ruia. "Thank you for your help. I could use my satchel off my horse."

"Will you be all right until I get back?"

"I think we've won this one, Ruia. You and your people should be proud."

She glanced around and shook her head. "I don't know about proud. It's enough to be alive."

He met her eyes and nodded in understanding, his respect for the girl deepening another notch. She held the look for a few heartbeats, then hurried off toward the screaming horses.

Tjety took a deep breath as Ruia's last words echoed in his mind. It *was* enough to be alive.

EZAGO SETTLED ONTO HIS camp cot, his legs stretched out and his hands folded onto his chest. He tugged on a simple blanket to keep his naked body warm, then closed his eyes. Several deep breaths had him slipping into a deep *hekau* meditative state, and then, carefully, he untethered his living ethereal *ba* from his body and spooled it out, soaring up through the cloth top of his tent and into the night sky.

He had no desire to exhaust himself unnecessarily, so he scanned around his surroundings until he found a likely carrier target and homed in on that. He streaked his *ba* toward the unsuspecting bird and slammed into it with the force of his *hekau*. This particular target was an owl, a larger example of the species than he usually encountered. The northern varieties of the bird were generally small. He guessed that frontier living resulted in larger, hardier birds.

As it was, it posed no threat to him, and its simple animal mind was easy to cordon off. He flexed his *hekau* and filled the living body of the bird with his *ba*, taking full possession of it from tail feathers to beak.

Zezago luxuriated in the feel of the wind buffeting his newfound wings; the rush of air over his beak and eyes. He settled into the senses and sensations the owl's body offered him, and wheeled into the air. He cut some lazy circles, getting used to the feeling of the body under his control. In particular, he took several deep cleansing breaths with its little lungs, cherishing the feel of a breath without the catch of a shuddering cough.

It had been far too long since he had taken flight. He made a mental note to himself to do this more often. Gliding up through the sky, fluttering over the treetops with this super light body under his control, reminded him of how hard it was to be a land-based human, chained to the same sickly body and limited to walking or riding.

But to fly! He flapped his wings and rose higher in the sky, caught a thermal and soared higher and higher, the mountain range far to the west coming into view as well as the blue ribbon of the great river snaking below him, curving far to the north and looping to the south. He could see so far from up here, even though this particular bird's eyes weren't as good as some others. Perhaps next time he would capture a hawk or an eagle, and…

He stopped his foolish thoughts. For now, on to business. He tucked in his wings and streaked down toward the ground, heading toward the rugged terrain the locals called the Dunes, crossing over that and moving toward the low foothills and rugged canyons between the quarry and the river. Somewhere down there was his caravan and his new shipment of slaves, and he was tired of relying on other people to deliver him information.

Sometimes you just had to take things in your own hands. Or wings, in this case. He laughed silently within the mind of the owl, sensing an animalistic, unfocused terror from the little corner of the beast's mind.

He glided over the trees, ruffling the very top branches with his passing. A nest of starlings took flight in a spray of feathers and indignant cheeps.

Reminded of an unfortunate moment in his past,

he siphoned off part of his *hekau* and used it to scan for possible threats. A hungry predator might pick him out for an easy target, and he had no desire to lose this body and get snapped back to his own body without due warning. The return would hurt, and he didn't have time to waste.

He braked his descent and banked through tall cedars lining the rough road through a series of switchbacks set into the hills leading toward the river, focusing his new eyes at the ground.

Just ahead a veritable swarm of carrion birds had started to gather. If he was careful, they would pay him no mind, thinking of him as another bird coming to join whatever party they were celebrating. He focused on the area below their circling, and a dark rage filled his mind.

His caravan was in shambles. Two covered wagons and one plain buckboard lay clustered along a swath of land that appeared to have been used as a campsite. Bodies of horses, his soldiers, some villagers, and most of his constructs lay sprawled as well, evidence of a recent bloody melee.

As he joined his other feathered cousins in wheeling around the impromptu battlefield, a deeply tanned, olive-skinned young man stood up from behind one of the wagons, a khopesh in his left hand gleaming in the moonlight. The man swung the weapon down to decapitate a construct flailing on the ground at his feet.

Zezago noted the awkwardness of the movement, then saw that the man's right arm was in a sling. Perhaps he'd been wounded. Interesting.

He continued to wheel around, taking in as much information as he could. A girl in a tattered dress rushed toward the young man with a satchel in her hands. When she handed it to the man, they touched hands, and when they did, their respective *hekau* flared in a brief flash of mystical energies. Zezago knew then and there that the man was a *hekau* practitioner of some unknown ability. And somehow that girl had vestiges of talent as well. Most interesting, indeed.

Curious, he angled in closer. The khopesh in the man's hands and the tangled headcloth wrapped around his wounded arm and chest suggested he was a servant of Kekhmet, one of Mayat's vaunted Rangers. The girl's *hekau* flared as well, though hers was far less bright than the Ranger's.

Zezago frowned, or frowned as best he could in his new skin. He didn't know what to make of the girl, but was curious to learn more. He lowered his wings and circled even closer to the action, diving lower than the other carrion birds.

From this closer vantage point, he saw a solitary survivor in familiar leathers slipping away from the battle, leading a horse through the thickest cluster of trees. Zezago focused in on that survivor and experienced mixed feelings. It was his foreman, Qebsenuf. That the man had survived the battle wasn't a great surprise—Qebsenuf was his most resourceful servant and a determined survivor to the core of his being. That he was apparently the *only* survivor, save for the odd construct that had wandered off into the trees chasing shadows, was more disturbing.

Qebsenuf mounted his horse and rode hard to the north, no doubt toward the quarry. Zezago continued to circle the campsite with the other birds, watching as the villagers gathered under the guidance of the young girl with the matted sidelock and the strangely fluttering *hekau*. She soon led them over to meet up with the Ranger.

Zezago let out a sigh that sounded like a plaintive hoot. These two would require closer attention.

He lifted himself up higher, his mood fluctuating as his mind raced with questions and possibilities.

What would the Ranger and the girl do now? Their home was in ruins, and with many of their fellow villagers dead or wounded, they wouldn't have enough people to turn the village into a going concern any more. They'd have to find a new life somewhere else.

His initial survey suggested many of them were wounded, some severely, including the Ranger with that bloody bandage on his arm. There were also several dead horses on the makeshift battlefield, and only a few that appeared capable of being pressed into service. Too few for all of the survivors to ride.

The fort, he decided. It was the only logical place for them to go. Situated in the hills overlooking a bend in the river, Fort Sekhmet was much closer than their broken village and the other, more northerly, fishing village that his men had already emptied and gutted. If that Ranger had any sense of the local terrain, which had to be likely, he would see the fort as the only real choice of destination.

Zezago nodded his little owl head. Yes, the fort is where the Ranger would lead this sad assembly of survivors. And on the road from here to there, his soldiers and his constructs would take them all.

Boldly, he angled down under the curious eyes

of carrion birds of all stripes, and in the moonlight found several of his feathered brethren perched upon a mighty cedar at the edge the campsite. He flared his wings, landed amongst the other birds, and then settled in. He rotated his head and focused his hateful stare upon the survivors, in particular that curious upstart Ranger.

WITH THE MOON AT full rise and peeking out from a thin spread of clouds, Tjety took a ragged breath and settled himself onto a makeshift bench near the fire pit in the center of the camp. He was bone-weary, and he ached all over, particularly the bullet wound in his arm.

Fucking thing had to be infected. He winced as he rubbed at the wound. Nothing to do for it now but to try and fix the worst of it. He had grabbed one of the metal tent spikes from the bandit supplies and stuck it into the fire.

He drew his small belt knife and sliced into the dirty scab that had built up around the wound, shoved a length of rope in between his teeth, and then reached out with his good hand bundled in his headcloth for the heated metal bar. He pulled it out of the fire and then held his breath as he pushed the red-hot end of it deep into his wound. He screamed around the rope in his mouth but focused with all his remaining *hekau* on the task at hand, working the metal bar around, burning out as much of the diseased flesh as he could.

At some point he must have passed out, because he woke up with Ruia shouting his name.

He roused and she knelt over him, the weariness in her body and eyes evident. "Oh, Tjety. What have you done?"

He lifted his good arm toward her, and she grabbed it and helped him up to a sitting position. "Did what I had to…to try and save my arm."

She sat down next to him and looked doubtfully at the still-hot length of metal. "Do you think it helped?"

He shook his head and with a shaky hand pulled a dented flask off the ground near his feet. "Damned if I know." He took a swig from the flask and then offered it to her.

She gave it an uncertain look. "What's that?"

He indicated she should drink. "Not sure, but it's got a nice warmth to it. I found it on one of the bandit's bodies." He stared into the fire. "He won't need it any more."

She gave him a look, then accepted the flask and took a sip. She flinched back and coughed.

"Gods, that's awful." She gave him a sour face, then handed the flask back to him. "You're right, though. It is warm." She rested one hand on her stomach. "I can feel the heat all the way down here."

He picked up his last length of clean bandages and tried to wind them around his wound, but fumbled with it and dropped the linen into the dirt. Ruia made a little clucking sound and knelt down next to him. She picked up the bandage, shook off the dirt, and started to wrap his wound.

"I don't know what to do next, Ranger. Some of my friends want to return home, back to the village."

"That'd be the fool's path." Tjety watched her as she bound his arm. "With maybe more of those unliving things out there and who knows what other frontier creatures lurking about, your people would never make it back to the village, not without suffering even more casualties."

Ruia gave him a sidelong glance. "Not if we had your gun and your help."

He snorted into the dirt. "You wouldn't get there

unscathed with a dozen Rangers helping you."

She frowned, frustration evident in the set of her shoulders and mouth. She tied off the bandage, making him wince with the tightness.

"That doesn't speak too well of the Rangers, does it? And it's not like you've been much help! You needed me to rescue you! Why aren't my people good enough for you to return the favor?" She stood up, shaking, her hands balled up into fists and pressed hard against her thighs.

He thought she'd take a swing at him; was surprised she managed to rein it in. He shook his head. "You take offense where none is offered, Ruia. My point is that going back to the village won't do you or your people any good. All that's left there is death and bad memories."

Tjety saw the tears in her eyes well up and looked away. How much more pain would he see? The look in her eyes reminded him again of Neferuta. Gods damn it all.

Ruia sat back down. After a long moment of staring into the fire, she asked, "What are we supposed to do? Where do we go?"

Tjety shook his head. "I don't know, Ruia. I really don't. I think the best thing is to make for Fort

Sekhmet. There we can get food, water, bandages…" He rubbed his wounded arm, nodded. "And maybe some answers. The soldiers there might know something about this band of brigands and those… creatures." He sighed, then added, "And I think there's a priest at the fort. They can help too."

Ruia thumbed a tear out of her eye. "So we go there for food and rest. What then?"

He shrugged. "Then you find a new life for yourself, I guess." He winced at the spears of heat in his wound and channeled some of his remaining *hekau* into blunting the worst of the pain. It wasn't much, but it helped.

Ruia crossed her arms and shivered. "But where? Maybe head for the city of the provincial governor? Report the attack on our village?"

Tjety spat into the dirt. "I bet the provincial governor hasn't taken a step out of his palace for years. Given the state of the frontier, I don't think he has a clue how tattered his domain is."

Ruia shook her head. "Or maybe he does know and just doesn't want to do anything to help us." She stared at him with hollow eyes. "I don't know anything about such things. I'm just a dumb girl from a fishing village."

He nudged her with his good hand. "Don't you say that. No, Ruia. You're far beyond that. You're someone special."

She scoffed. "Special how?"

Tjety screwed on the cap to the flask and shoved it into his satchel. He reached out with a tendril of his tired *hekau* to touch her *ba*. "You're a survivor, Ruia. And that means a lot. Think about what you've been through over the last few days. Think about all your friends and family who weren't so fortunate. You survived all that, and here you are."

She pulled her knees up to her chin and wrapped her arms around herself. "Yeah, here I am. Nowhere."

He shook his head. "Nah, you're here, and you're alive. Don't take that for granted. No matter how beat up you are, no matter how sore your body, you're still alive and able to fight another day." He stared at her, confirmed his guess with a tendril of thought, then shut down his *hekau* so he could rest. "And there's something else. You have some *hekau* talent about you. Remember your amulet, and your vision of the Lady Mayat?"

She turned disbelieving eyes on him. "What?"

Tjety raised his chin toward her. "How did you get away from the bandits in the first place? How did you get through their camp and into the trees?"

"I've always been good at hiding." Ruia glanced at him and then focused on the fire. "I was always the winner in the sneaking games the children played in the village. I once hid for two days straight. They never found me."

"That's not just luck, Ruia." He reached out and gently turned her chin to face him. "That takes a talent a lot of people don't have, and a talent it takes years to master. It's the *hekau*. The life-force that dwells within all of us. Some of us can learn to use it, in a variety of ways." He touched his chest. "I'm shit at not being seen. I just don't have the talent for it." He offered a wan smile. "Though my trainers would suggest that I just didn't have the patience."

She frowned. "The patience for what?"

"To be trained." He stared at her. "Ranger training teaches us a lot of things. Not just how to shoot a gun or swing a blade, but how to sense things others can't sense, how to look into the hearts and minds of men and women, how to navigate the paths between right and wrong. All through the strength of our *hekau*."

She shook her head and focused again on the dying fire. "I don't know such things. I can cook bread, skin a fish, and occasionally hide from other children. No one in my village knows anything about any *hekau*."

Tjety reached out a tentative hand and rested it on her shoulder. "Someone did." He reached a finger out and hooked the simple necklace that supported her lapis amulet. "Who gave you this?"

She glanced down, and defensively cupped a hand around the amulet. "My ma."

He dropped his hand back to his lap. "She knew something about *hekau*. Couldn't be a coincidence. That's a centering amulet, Ruia. Students new to the mysteries use them to focus their *hekau*. Most grow out of using them, but sometimes they hang onto them."

Ruia stared at him with wonder and sorrow in her eyes, then glanced down into her hand at the amulet. "My ma knew?"

Tjety nodded, even though she didn't see. "She must have known you had some talent, more than the other children." He nudged her. "The whispers in your head. How long have you heard them?"

She leaned away. "I haven't heard any voices."

He snorted. "Horseshit. You told me you did." He offered her a smile. "Come on, how long?"

She met his eyes and then stared into the fire again. "A year? Maybe more. On and off, only on occasion. Stronger lately, including that thing with the Lady Mayat. That was the loudest they've been."

"It's the gods, you know. Talking to us, helping us. Hard to understand them, to figure out what the fuck they want. But, you can learn to quiet them in time. Even without training. Just, focus on what you want your *hekau* to do, and with practice, you'll be able to use your abilities without hearing the voices."

Ruia dropped her chin to her chest. "I don't know such things. I'm just a fisherman's daughter."

Tjety slapped his good hand against the ground. "You're more than that! Or, at least, you have the potential to be much more. If you want it, anyway." He clenched a hand to his chest. "I can *feel* it." And then, for a moment, his spirit lightened. "You remind me of someone, you know."

She glanced at him. "Who do I remind you of, Ranger?"

He smiled, the connection fusing in his mind. "My sister. Neferuta. She's a survivor too. And she's tough, like you, and smart as a whip."

Ruia met his eyes, curiosity shining in them. "She a Ranger too?"

He shook his head. "No, fuck, no. She was too smart to join the Rangers. She joined the priesthood, actually. Started off as a priestess of Pakhet but is probably a Daughter of Isis now. She has more of a mind for politics than I ever want to bother with."

"You miss her." The statement was flat, not a question.

Tjety stared at her, then back to the fire. "I…I don't know. I guess so. The last time we talked—we had an argument. She won, of course, but I was too full of piss and pride to admit it. I stormed off, she stormed off, and we haven't talked since. Been a couple years now."

Ruia stared into the fire for a time, sitting with him in something resembling companionable silence, then sighed and slowly stood up. She glanced down at him. "I'll talk to my friends. If you can help us get to the fort, I'd be grateful, for all of us." She shrugged. "For whatever that's worth."

He met her eyes and pushed himself up to his feet. He reached out and took her hands in his good hand. "Ruia, by my commission as a Ranger of Mayat and as a hopeful new friend, I promise to get you all to Fort Sekhmet or die in the trying."

She stared at him over their clasped hands, then gave him a tired smile. She then let go of his hand

and headed for the covered wagon that had been converted into a sleeping den.

Tjety watched her disappear into the darkness, and then adjusted his sling and stood up. He moved over to the picket line and busied himself with tending to Heker, taking some time with his beloved horse after all that had transpired.

He then grabbed his bedroll and found a clear spot of ground to spread out upon. He raised his weary eyes to the rising moon. After musing over divine Khonsu's glow for a time, he turned his focus onto a bunch of birds preening on one of the large cedars at the outskirts of camp. A mix of birds hopped from branch to branch, grousing at each other for space or for dominance or for something beyond his understanding.

One of the birds in particular caught his attention. As he focused on it, a strange shiver rippled through his *hekau*. The bird, a massive brown owl, stared at him with hard, unblinking eyes.

He frowned, sensing something distinctly unnatural about that bird. The feeling was unlike anything he'd experienced before, and the more he focused on it, the more he realized he hated the fearful crawlings it rose up in him. He drifted his hand down toward his pistol grip, but then checked himself. He had better things to do than let himself get spooked over some gods-damned dirty bird. He reached down for a small rock and tossed it toward the birds. Most of them scattered. Except for that big owl.

The bird tilted its head to and fro as it stared at him, as if taking his full measure. Finally, with a powerful sweep of its wings, it launched into the air.

Tjety's eyes followed the strange bird as it wheeled up, higher and higher, until its dark form blended into the dark sky and disappeared from sight. He stared at the multitude of stars above, wondering if his exile to the frontier had been a blessing in disguise, or a curse for all time.

The adventures of Tjety and Ruia continue in
Pistols and Pyramids #2:

AFTERWORD

I've been an avid fan of Westerns since I was a little 'un, particularly those on television and the big screen. I read my share of Louis L'Amour and Zane Grey and the various and sundry series out there, but it was the television and movie Westerns that really captured my imagination. You'll have no doubt noted that this book and series is also heavily influenced and inspired by ancient Egyptian mythology, something I've had an interest in for most of my adult life. There aren't many stories out there that combine the traditional American Western with ancient Egyptian culture and mythology, which seems odd to me. (If you know of any, please drop me a note at jim@scribeineti.com and let me know. I'd love to hear about them.)

You may also note that I've played it pretty fast and loose with both the traditional Western tropes and the ancient Egyptian elements. If you're a student of either and note discrepancies between this story and reality, please remember that this is a piece of fiction, and not even historical fiction at that. I think I got most of the details fairly right, but the ones I didn't are either a gaffe on my part or an intentional alteration of what's in the history and archaeology books. Either way, I hope you enjoyed your time in Kekhmet, and truly hope you'll return. You'll always be welcome.

So, thanks so much for picking up this book and trying it out. I hope you enjoyed reading it as much as I did writing it. May your horse be sound, your aim be true, and your scales be always in balance.

Jim Johnson
October 2015
Alexandria, VA

ACKNOWLEDGMENTS

This book took a team to put together, and this is my opportunity to thank that team. First, to my editor Erica Satifka, who provided critical commentary on the manuscript and whose efforts made this book and series far stronger. To my cover artist, print layout guru, friend, and fellow Literary Outlaw, Kevin G. Summers, who patiently worked with me through dozens of emails and Facebook conversations to get the cover text and layout just right. To artist James Hale, for providing the fantastic illustrations in this book--the sketches and final product provided a huge jolt of inspiration to my own humble hekau. And to my team of beta readers, thank you for your efforts. I didn't use all of your comments, but I hope I used the right ones. Your advice made this a better book.

Thanks to the members and participants of sundry online writing communities out there, including the Pulp Speeders, denizens of kboards' Writer's Cafe, the SFWA forums, and many others. I've learned from you all and have drawn inspiration from you all as well. Also thanks to Marco Palmieri, who reviewed a pre-alpha draft of this story and provided a treasure trove of good advice that shaped my thoughts on the series moving forward.

Special thanks to composers John Barry (*Dances With Wolves*), Jeff Beal (*Appaloosa*), Marco Beltrami (*3:10 to Yuma*), Bruce Broughton (*Tombstone*), Nick Cave & Warren Ellis (*The Assassination of Jesse James by the Coward Robert Ford*), Bill Elm and Woody Jackson (*Red Dead Redemption* and *Red Dead Redemption: Undead Nightmare*), James Newton Howard (*Wyatt Earp*), Kevin Kiner & Gustavo Santaolalla (*Hell on Wheels*), Ennio Morricone (too many to list), Lennie Niehaus (*Unforgiven*), Alan Silvestri (*The Quick and the Dead*), Keith Zizza (*Pharaoh, Children of the Nile)* and all of the musicians who worked with them on their respective scores and soundtracks. Your music was and is a constant inspiration during the development and writing of this series. Thank you all.

To my son Jacob Robert, born just a few weeks before I hit the 'Publish' button on the first book in this series, I love you, son. This book is the first piece of your legacy, and I sure hope you enjoy it when you're old enough to read it.

And finally, to my wife Damaris: thank you for your love, your support, and your confidence in my efforts. I'm grateful you're with me on this crazy journey. Love you much, my dear.

ABOUT THE AUTHOR

Jim Johnson is the author of the *Pistols and Pyramids* series as well as other prose fiction series currently under development. He has written sundry other pieces of fiction, including several stories published in the *Star Trek* universe, and has freelanced for pen and paper roleplaying game companies, including Decipher and White Wolf. Please visit www.SCRIBEINETI.com for more information on Jim and his interests and writing.

When he is not busy writing and publishing and reading, Jim can be found catering to the Cat Overlords' collective demands; tinkering with LEGO brick creations; playing various console, board, and card games; contra dancing; playing djembe in a drum circle; listening to movie/television soundtracks and rap/hip-hop albums; and occasionally working with various community theater groups in the DC metro area. He may also be found catching a movie at the Alamo Drafthouse.

Jim lives in historic Alexandria, VA with his wife, newborn son, and several crazy cats.